General Educational Development Testing Se[...]
A Program of the American Council on Edu[...]

Dear GED Candidate:

Congratulations on taking one of the most important steps of your life—earning a GED credential!

Since 1942, millions of people like you have taken the GED Tests to continue their education, to get a better job, or to achieve a sense of accomplishment.

We are delighted to introduce **Keys to GED® Success: Language Arts, Writing**—an invaluable resource to help you pass the GED Language Arts, Writing Test. It has been developed through a partnership between the GED Testing Service®–developer of the GED Tests–and Steck-Vaughn, a leading provider of GED test preparation materials and the exclusive distributor of the Official GED Practice Tests.

GEDTS researched the types of skills that GED candidates could focus on to improve their chances of passing the tests. We identified the types of questions and possible reasons that test-takers were missing specific questions on each test and decided to share that information. GEDTS collaborated with Steck-Vaughn to target those skills in a workbook that would benefit present and future GED candidates. The skills targeted in our research are called the **GED® Key Skills**—which is what you'll find in this book. In addition to the **GED Key Skills**, this book includes other important lessons that are needed to pass the GED Language Arts, Writing Test.

To help GED teachers, there is a Teaching Tips section included. The tips are written to address teaching strategies for some of the key problem areas that emerged from our research.

As the owner of this book, you can use the Pretest to determine exactly which skills you need to target to pass the test. Once you have completed your study, you can determine whether you are ready to take the GED Language Arts, Writing Test by taking an Official GED Practice Test—which follows Lesson 20. The GED Testing Service has developed this practice test as a predictor of the score that you will likely earn on the actual GED Language Arts, Writing Test.

Remember that there are four other books in the **Keys to GED Success** series. These other books cover the remaining four GED Tests: Language Arts, Reading, Science, Social Studies, and Mathematics. All titles in this series are available exclusively from Steck-Vaughn.

We wish you the best of luck on the GED Tests.

Sylvia E. Robinson
Executive Director
GED® Testing Service

September 2008

STECK-VAUGHN

Keys to GED® SUCCESS

Language Arts, Writing

Steck
Vaughn™

HOUGHTON MIFFLIN HARCOURT
Supplemental Publishers

www.SteckVaughn.com/AdultEd
800-531-5015

ISBN-10:   1-4190-5348-5
ISBN-13: 978-1-4190-5348-1

5 6 7 8 9 1689 15 14 13 12 11

4500311236

[Contents]

KEY This symbol indicates *GED* ® *Key Skills* as identified by the GED Testing Service ®.

Using This Book

Keys to GED₀ Success: Language Arts, Writing has been prepared by Steck-Vaughn in cooperation with the GED Testing Service₀. This book focuses on the thinking skills needed to pass the GED Language Arts, Writing Test.

This book also identifies the *GED₀ Key Skills*, which are skills that the GED Testing Service₀ has pinpointed as those most often missed by test takers who come close to passing the GED Tests. For more information about these skills see *A Message from the GED Testing Service₀* at the front of this book.

In this book, the *GED Key Skills* are identified by this symbol: **KEY**

It is recommended that students who are preparing to take the GED Tests follow this plan:

1. Take the Language Arts, Writing Pretest.

While it is best to work through all the lessons in this book, students can choose to focus on specific skills. The *Language Arts, Writing Pretest* assesses the 20 skills in this book. The *Pretest Performance Analysis Chart* on page 9 will help students to target the skills that need the most attention.

2. Work through the 4-page skill lessons in the book.

• The first page of each lesson provides an approach to the skill and to thinking through the questions. Students should carefully read the step-by-step thinking strategies and pay attention to the explanations of why the correct answers are right and why the wrong answer choices are incorrect.

• The second page of each lesson contains sample GED questions. Students should use the hints and the answers and explanations sections to improve their understanding of how to answer questions about each skill.

• The third and fourth pages of each lesson present GED practice questions that allow students to apply the skill to the same types of questions that they will see on the test.

Students should use the *Answers and Explanations* at the back of this book to check their answers and to learn more about how to make the correct answer choices.

3. Take the *Official GED® Practice Test Form PA: Language Arts, Writing* in this book and analyze the results.

The half-length practice test at the end of this book is the Official GED Practice Test Form PA: Language Arts, Writing–developed by the GED Testing Service®. Taking this test allows students to evaluate how well they will do on the actual GED Language Arts, Writing Test.

Based on the results, test administrators can determine if the student is ready to take the actual test. Those students who are not ready will need more study and should use the other GED Language Arts, Writing preparation materials available from Steck-Vaughn, which are listed at the back of this book and can be found at www.SteckVaughn.com/AdultEd.

4. Prior to taking the GED Language Arts, Writing Test, take an additional Official GED Practice Test.

The more experience that students have taking practice tests, the better they will do on the actual test. For additional test practice, they can take the Full-Length Practice Test Form or any of the other Official GED Practice Tests available from Steck-Vaughn at www.SteckVaughn.com/AdultEd.

By using this book and the others in this series, students will have the information and strategies developed by both the GED Testing Service® and experienced adult educators, so that they can reach their goal—passing the GED Tests.

Teaching Tips

Below are suggested interactive teaching strategies that support and develop specific **GED® Key Skills**.

Combining Sentences (Language Arts, Writing KEY Skill 4)

Discuss that two clauses (groups of words with subjects and verbs that express a complete thought) can be combined if: 1) the clauses are combined correctly with a comma and a conjunction and 2) the new sentence makes sense. Use an example to illustrate: *Lila's job is being eliminated by her company. She needs to find a new one soon.*

- Combine the clauses with a commas and coordinating conjunctions (*for, and, nor, but, or, yet, so*), and discuss which conjunctions create sentences that make sense.

- Combine the clauses with commas and subordinating conjunctions (*although, before, because, if, since, unless, until, while*), and discuss which conjunctions create sentences that make sense.

- Generate two related simple sentences, and find as many ways as possible to combine them to make sense using coordinating conjunctions and subordinating conjunctions. Use punctuation correctly.

ESSAY LINK: *The score on a student's essay will be favorably influenced by the correct use of compound and complex sentences. Reinforce the importance of using compound and complex sentences instead of simple sentences when reviewing student writing.*

Spelling Homonyms (Language Arts, Writing KEY Skill 15)

Discuss that homonyms are words that sound the same but have different meanings and spellings.

- Use examples like: *weak* and *week* or *here* and *hear*. Review the difference in spelling and meaning between possessive pronouns and their corresponding homonyms (*its/it's, theirs/there's*).

- Based on a list of commonly confused homonyms (including their meanings), write homonyms on slips of paper and put the slips in containers for pairs of students. One student from each pair picks a paper with homonyms and writes two sentences using the homonyms correctly. The other student either agrees or disagrees with its usage. Students can consult the master list that you worked from or a dictionary if there is a dispute.

- The process is repeated with the other student and continues until the container is empty.

ESSAY LINK: *In their writing, students often confuse common homonyms such as too/to/two, its/it's, and there/their/they're. Remind students that they can make a good impression on the readers who score their essays if they carefully proofread their work and <u>neatly</u> correct these common mistakes during proofreading.*

Irrelevant Sentences (Language Arts, Writing KEY Skill 18)

Discuss that paragraphs are based on one main idea. On the GED Language Arts, Writing Test, test takers may have to answer multiple-choice questions that require them to "remove" a sentence that does not support the main idea of the paragraph.

- Locate a well-written paragraph of 5–7 sentences that contains a clearly stated main idea and supporting sentences.

- Decide what the topic of the paragraph is. For example, the topic could be "looking for the lowest gas prices."

- Type up the paragraph, and insert a sentence that is somewhat related to the paragraph but is extraneous to the topic of the paragraph, for instance, "I have been driving the same car for 7 years."

- Read the paragraph and discuss the following questions: *What is the paragraph about?* (Narrow the focus, if the response is general, like 'cars' or 'gas.') *Which sentence should be removed because it does not support the topic of this paragraph?*

ESSAY LINK: *Remind students to keep the idea of relevant sentences in mind when they write their essays. When they are finished writing their essays, they should reread them. If a paragraph has a clearly irrelevant sentence, they can <u>neatly</u> cross it out. The readers who score their papers will appreciate that they kept their paragraphs "on topic."*

Language Arts, Writing Pretest

Directions

This pretest consists of 20 questions designed to measure how well you know the skills needed to pass the GED Language Arts, Writing Test. There is one question for each of the 20 lessons in this book.

- Take the pretest and record your answers on the *Pretest Answer Sheet* found on page 123. Choose the one best answer to each question.

- Check your answers in the *Pretest Answers and Explanations* section, which starts on page 107. Reading the explanations for the answers will help you understand why the correct answers are right and the incorrect answer choices are wrong.

- Fill in the *Pretest Performance Analysis Chart* on page 9 to determine which skills are the most important for you to focus on as you work in this book.

....

Questions 1 through 4 refer to the following paragraph.

(1) Almost all electronic appliances, from microwave ovens to DVD players, uses circuit boards. (2) Circuit boards vary in complexity, but all contain instruction panels composed of integrated circuits, resistors, capacitors, and other electrical components. (3) These components were connected by conducting paths. (4) The panels tell the machine what to do by conducting electrical current along pathways. (5) These circuit boards are manufactured by using highly toxic acids to conduct electricity over copper-coated panels. (6) When the boards are overused. (7) The copper overheats and stops the electrical current. (8) It is the most common cause of malfunction in household appliances.

1. Sentence 1: **Almost all electronic appliances, from microwave ovens to DVD players, uses circuit boards.**

   Which correction should be made to sentence 1?

   (1) replace <u>all</u> with <u>every</u>
   (2) insert a comma after <u>all</u>
   (3) remove the comma after <u>appliances</u>
   (4) change <u>uses</u> to <u>use</u>
   (5) no correction is necessary

2. Sentence 3: **These components were connected by conducting paths.**

   Which correction should be made to sentence 3?

   (1) insert a comma after <u>components</u>
   (2) replace <u>were</u> with <u>are</u>
   (3) remove <u>conducting</u>
   (4) replace <u>paths</u> with <u>path's</u>
   (5) no correction is necessary

3. Sentences 6 and 7: **When the boards <u>are overused. The copper</u> overheats and stops the electrical current.**

   Which is the <u>best</u> way to write the underlined portion of these sentences? If the original is the best way, choose option (1).

   (1) are overused. The copper
   (2) are overused the copper
   (3) are overused so the copper
   (4) are overused and the copper
   (5) are overused, the copper

4. Sentence 8: **It is the most common cause of malfunction in household appliances.**

   Which correction should be made to sentence 8?

   (1) replace <u>It</u> with <u>This overheating</u>
   (2) replace <u>It</u> with <u>That</u>
   (3) insert <u>single</u> before <u>most</u>
   (4) insert <u>these</u> before <u>household</u>
   (5) no correction is necessary

Questions 5 through 10 refer to the following passage.

How to Make a Child's Trip to the Emergency Room Less Stressful

(A)

(1) Emergency rooms in the United States are increasingly busy places. (2) A considerable portion of the business of emergency rooms are treating children. (3) Each year the staffs of hospital emergency rooms treat more than 25 million children who are in distress. (4) The most common reasons children are taken to hospitals are trauma (an injury or accident), infectious diseases (such as the flu), or a chronic illness (such as asthma). (5) Whenever a child is taken to the hospital, the experience can be as frightening for the parent as for the child. (6) It is important to try to remain calm in order to make appropriate decisions regarding your child's care. (7) Hospital personnel encourage parents to stay with their children to provide emotional support.

(B)

(8) Although you are anxious, you need to focus on the child. (9) The child needs to be reassured. (10) The child takes cues from parents on how to react to situations. (11) If you are hysterical, your child may become more frightened from your reaction than from his or her actual discomfort. (12) You also need to be patient, there is going to be a certain amount of waiting and paperwork to deal with, even in emergency cases. (13) Naturally, you want your child to be cared for immediately, and hospital personnel are trained to make quick decisions. (14) In some cases, you may be separated from the child for a while. (15) If you must part for a few minutes, reassure the child that the hospital staff will take good care of him or her.

(C)

(16) Be sure to do nothing that will contribute to a feeling of fear. (17) Many soldiers say that fear is paralyzing. (18) Talk to your child in a soft voice, and explain what is happening. (19) Your composed confidence will go a long way toward helping the child. (20) Don't be afraid to ask questions, but remember that hospital personnel are trained for these situations. (21) Your participation will help the hospital staff treat your child quickly and safely. (22) No parent wants to think of his or her children becoming sick or injured, but when they are, a parent can be most helpful by remaining calm.

5. Sentence 2: **A considerable portion of the business of emergency rooms are treating children.**

   Which correction should be made to sentence 2?

   (1) replace <u>portion</u> with <u>part</u>
   (2) insert a comma after <u>rooms</u>
   (3) change <u>are</u> to <u>is</u>
   (4) remove <u>of the business</u>
   (5) no correction is necessary

6. Which revision would most improve the effectiveness of paragraph A?

   Begin a new paragraph with

   (1) sentence 4
   (2) sentence 5
   (3) sentence 6
   (4) sentence 7
   (5) no revision is necessary

7. Sentence 7: **When they can hospital personnel encourage parents to stay with their children to provide emotional support.**

Which correction should be made to sentence 7?

(1) insert a comma after <u>can</u>
(2) change <u>encourage</u> to <u>encourages</u>
(3) change <u>their</u> to <u>they're</u>
(4) insert a comma after <u>children</u>
(5) no correction is necessary

8. Which is the most effective rewrite of sentences 8, 9, and 10?

(1) Although you are anxious, you need to focus on the child, which needs to be reassured. The child takes cues from parents on how to react to situations.
(2) Although you are anxious, you need to focus on the child, the child needs to be reassured. The child takes cues from parents on how to react to situations.
(3) Although anxious, the child needs to be reassured, and focus gives cues on how to react to situations.
(4) Although you are anxious, you need to focus on the child, who needs to be reassured and takes cues from parents on how to react to situations.
(5) no revision is necessary

9. Sentence 12: **You also <u>need to be patient, there is</u> going to be a certain amount of waiting and paperwork to deal with, even in emergency cases.**

Which is the <u>best</u> way to write the underlined portion of this sentence? If the original is the best way, choose option (1).

(1) need to be patient, there is
(2) need to be patient, and there
(3) need to be patient there is
(4) need to be patient; however there is
(5) need to be patient. There is

10. Which of these sentences from paragraph C should be removed from the paragraph?

(1) Be sure to do nothing that will contribute to a feeling of fear. (sentence 16)
(2) Many soldiers say that fear is paralyzing. (sentence 17)
(3) Talk to your child in a soft voice, and explain what is happening. (sentence 18)
(4) Don't be afraid to ask questions, but remember that hospital personnel are trained for these situations. (sentence 20)
(5) Your participation will help the hospital staff treat your child quickly and safely. (sentence 21)

MEMORANDUM

September 14, 2009

To: All employees
From: J. Mosley, Human Resource
Re: Computer System Upgrade

(A)

(1) As you know, Morton Billing Systems will be introducing an upgraded computer system into all departments this will happen over the course of about the next six weeks. (2) This upgrade will affect all employees who work with computers on our in-house network.

(B)

(3) We will hold training sessions that will very from department to department. (4) During group training, your new systems will be installed, so prepare your workspaces accordingly. (5) It is critical that all employees participate in these training sessions. (6) In addition to upgraded computer hardware, new software is included with the machines. (7) This new software includes new network logon and security procedures as well as new data screens, which you will need to do your job. (8) Data entry will be streamlined with user-friendly screens and upgraded graphics.

(C)

(9) After initial training, a team of trainers from the computer vendor will spend a week in each department to answer questions and deal with any problems that might arise during the cutover period. (10) Once the systems are up and running smoothly, problems were met with a phone call to a service hotline that will be available 16 hours a day. (11) Cutover will be gradual, with departments phased in and brought online weekly.

(D)

(12) You will soon receive a schedule showing the dates for your departments two-week training period. (13) We think the benefits of the new system will be evident to all. (14) We are confident that with your cooperation, the transition will run smoothly.

11. Sentence 1: **As you know, Morton Billing Systems will be introducing an upgraded computer system into <u>all departments this will happen</u> over the course of about the next six weeks.**

Which is the <u>best</u> way to write the underlined portion of this sentence? If the original is the best way, choose option (1).

(1) all departments this will happen
(2) all departments, this will happen
(3) all departments. This will happen
(4) all departments when this will happen
(5) all departments, which this will happen

12. Sentence 3: **We will hold training sessions that will very from department to department.**

Which correction should be made to sentence 3?

(1) replace <u>will hold</u> with <u>will be holding</u>
(2) replace <u>very</u> with <u>vary</u>
(3) replace <u>from</u> with <u>to</u>
(4) replace <u>to</u> with <u>and</u>
(5) no correction is necessary

13. Sentence 10: **Once the systems are up and <u>running smoothly, problems were met</u> with a phone call to a service hotline that will be available 16 hours a day.**

Which is the <u>best</u> way to write the underlined portion of this sentence? If the original is the best way, choose option (1).

(1) running smoothly, problems were met
(2) running smoothly. Problems were met
(3) running smoothly problems were met
(4) running smoothly, problems will be met
(5) running smoothly problems are met

14. Sentence 12: **You will soon receive a schedule showing the dates for your departments two-week training period.**

Which correction should be made to sentence 12?

(1) change <u>departments</u> to <u>department's</u>
(2) change <u>your</u> to <u>you're</u>
(3) change <u>two-week</u> to <u>two-weeks</u>
(4) change <u>departments</u> to <u>departments'</u>
(5) no correction is necessary

Alonzo Rodriguez
1423 River Drive
Atlanta, GA 30384

Mr. Martin Paulsen   August 12, 2009
Board of Education
Richmond, VA 23217

Dear Mr. Paulsen:

(A)

(1) I am writing in response to the advertisement I saw in the Sunday newspaper for the position of peer counseling administrator. (2) I believe I would be an excellent candidate for this position. (3) I have enclosed my resumé for your review.

(B)

(4) I have been a high school gym teacher for three years here in Atlanta. (5) Many local families are from other countries, and are unfamiliar with the American education system. (6) To help families such as these, I developed workshops for parents on how to communicate with the school and help children do homework. (7) Finally, I have run programs in conflict resolution and conducted training sessions for both teachers and students. (8) I also started a conflict resolution training program for parents to help they strengthen relationships with their own children. (9) The keys to the program were active listening, careful restating, and to withhold judgment. (10) These are the beliefs and skills I would bring to the position of peer counseling administrator.

(C)

(11) In addition to my experience, you will see that I have excellent recommendations from the principal of my school as well as other administrators.

(D)

(12) I will contact you in a few days to confirm receipt of my resumé. (13) Thank you for considering me.

Sincerely,

Alonzo Rodriguez

Alonzo Rodriguez

15. Sentence 7: **Finally, I have run programs in conflict resolution and conducted training sessions for both teachers and students.**

    Which is the <u>best</u> way to write the underlined portion of this sentence? If the original is the best way, choose option (1).

    (1) Finally, I have run programs
    (2) Finally, I had run programs
    (3) I will run programs
    (4) Whenever I have run programs,
    (5) In addition, I have run programs

16. Sentence 8: **I also started a conflict resolution training program for parents to help they strengthen relationships with their own children.**

    Which correction should be made to sentence 8?

    (1) insert comma after <u>parents</u>
    (2) replace <u>they</u> with <u>them</u>
    (3) replace <u>their</u> with <u>they're</u>
    (4) insert comma after <u>relationships</u>
    (5) no correction is necessary

17. Which is the most effective rewrite of sentence 9?

    (1) The keys to the program was active listening, careful restating, and to withhold judgment.
    (2) The keys to the program were active listening, careful restating, and withholding judgment.
    (3) The keys to the program were, active listening, careful restating, and to withhold judgment.
    (4) The keys to the programs were listening, restating, and judging.
    (5) The keys to the program were to listen actively, restate carefully, and withholding judgment.

18. Which revision would improve the effectiveness of paragraphs (C) and (D)?

    (1) reverse the order of the two paragraphs
    (2) remove paragraph (C)
    (3) combine (C) and (D) into a single paragraph
    (4) remove paragraph (D)
    (5) reverse the order of sentences 12 and 13

Stress and You

(1) When you're relaxed, your heart and rate of breathing slow down. (2) Blood pressure declines. (3) By learning how relax—truly relax—for just ten minutes a day, you can lower your stress level and gain more energy. (4) You can control your stress instead of allowing your stress to control you. (5) There are many different ways of relaxing. (6) Some people find, that vigorous exercising relaxes them. (7) Others prefer more meditative practices such as yoga or tai chi or visualizing peaceful situations. (8) Whatever works for you is fine. (9) But it is important in a busy world to find a way to relax, decompress, and lose your stress.

19. Sentence 6: **Some people find, that vigorous exercising relaxes them.**

    Which correction should be made to sentence 6?

    (1) remove comma after <u>find</u>
    (2) change <u>find</u> to <u>had found</u>
    (3) insert comma after <u>vigorous</u>
    (4) change <u>them</u> to <u>themselves</u>
    (5) no correction is necessary

20. Which sentence would be most effective if inserted at the beginning of the paragraph?

    (1) Stress can kill you.
    (2) It is impossible to avoid stress.
    (3) I personally fight stress by relaxing.
    (4) The way to relax is different for every person.
    (5) The key to controlling stress is to relax.

Pretest Performance Analysis Chart

The following chart can help you to determine your strengths and weaknesses on the skill areas needed to pass the GED Language Arts, Writing Test.

- Use the *Pretest Answers and Explanations* on pages 107–108 to check your answers.
- On the chart below:
    - Circle the question numbers that you answered correctly.
    - Put a check mark (✓) next to the skills for which you answered the questions incorrectly.
    - Use the page numbers to find the lessons that you need to target as you work.

Question Number	Skills to Target (✓)	GED Language Arts, Writing Skill Lessons	Page Numbers
3		**Skill 1:** Sentence Fragments	10–13
11		**Skill 2:** Run-On Sentences	14–17
9		**Skill 3:** Comma Splices	18–21
8		**Skill 4:** Combining Sentences	22–25
17		**Skill 5:** Parallel Structure	26–29
2		**Skill 6:** Verb Tenses	30–33
13		**Skill 7:** Sequence of Tenses	34–37
1		**Skill 8:** Subject-Verb Agreement	38–41
5		**Skill 9:** Common Agreement Problems	42–45
16		**Skill 10:** Pronouns	46–49
4		**Skill 11:** Pronouns and Antecedents	50–53
14		**Skill 12:** Apostrophes	54–57
7		**Skill 13:** Commas in Sentences	58–61
19		**Skill 14:** Unnecessary Commas	62–65
12		**Skill 15:** Spelling Homonyms	66–69
20		**Skill 16:** Topic Sentences	70–73
15		**Skill 17:** Transition Words	74–77
10		**Skill 18:** Irrelevant Sentences	78–81
6		**Skill 19:** Text Divisions Within Paragraphs	82–85
18		**Skill 20:** Text Divisions Within Documents	86–89

Sentence Fragments

Sentence fragments are common writing errors. Sentence fragments occur when an incomplete thought is written as if it were a complete sentence. Most fragments are missing a **subject**, a **verb**, or both.

Sentence Fragment: Before the war.

(Complete sentence: Before the war, life was pleasant.)

One type of fragment occurs when a **dependent clause** is separated from its **independent clause**. The fragment has a subject or a verb, but begins with a **subordinate conjunction**.

> <u>Although</u> the night was beautiful. It was cold.
> (Complete sentence: Although the night was beautiful, it was cold.)

You can correct a sentence fragment in several ways.

Method 1: Supply a subject or a verb to make a complete thought.

> **Fragment:** Rushing like a maniac to the car, late as usual.
> <u>I</u> was rushing like a maniac to the car, late as usual. *or*
> Rushing like a maniac to the car, I <u>was</u> late as usual.

Method 2: Join dependent and independent clauses with a comma.

> **Fragment:** Whenever I regret the past. I focus on the present and future.
> Whenever I regret the <u>past, I</u> focus on the present and future.

Method 3: Combine sentence fragments with related sentences to form complete ideas.

> **Fragment:** The music on the radio today. It is often an expression of anger.
> The music on the radio <u>today is often</u> an expression of anger.

Read the words below. Choose the <u>one best answer</u> to the question.

On a beautiful sunny morning with high hopes.

QUESTION: Which of the following corrections forms a complete sentence?

   (1) On a beautiful sunny, morning with high hopes.
   (2) With high hopes on a beautiful, sunny morning.
   (3) I left for work with high hopes on a beautiful, sunny morning.
   (4) To work with high hopes on a beautiful, sunny morning.
   (5) No correction is necessary.

EXPLANATIONS

   (1) No. The addition of a comma doesn't help. The fragment does not have a subject or a verb.
   (2) No. The order is changed, but the fragment still lacks a subject and a verb.
   (3) **Yes. Adding a subject (*I*) and verb (*left*) forms a complete thought.**
   (4) No. Although there is more information, there is still no subject or verb.
   (5) No. The fragment is an incomplete thought and lacks a subject and a verb.

ANSWER: (3) I left for work with high hopes on a beautiful, sunny morning.

Practice the Skill

Try these examples. Choose the one best answer to each question. Then check your answers and read the explanations.

(1) Celebrities such as movie stars, royalty, and rock bands often have difficulty living private lives. (2) So many photographers and fans. (3) They invade a star's privacy. (4) The public demands to know about personal milestones such as marriage or the birth of children. (5) Tragedies such as serious illness or even death not private.

1. Sentences 2 and 3: **So many photographers and <u>fans. They invade</u> a star's privacy.**

   Which is the <u>best</u> way to write the underlined portion of these sentences? If the original option is the best way, choose option (1).

   (1) fans. They invade
   (2) fans. They invaded
   (3) fans, they invade
   (4) fans; invade
   (5) fans invade

   HINT Do both sentences have complete subjects and verbs? If not, how could you combine them into a single complete thought?

2. Sentence 5: **Tragedies such as serious illness or even <u>death not</u> private.**

   Which is the <u>best</u> way to write the underlined portion of this sentence? If the original is the best way, choose option (1).

   (1) death not
   (2) death. They are not
   (3) death are not
   (4) death; they are not
   (5) death, they are not

   HINT Does the sentence have both a subject and a verb? If not, how could you write the sentence to make a complete thought?

Answers and Explanations

1. (5) fans invade
Option (5) is correct because it combines two related thoughts into a complete sentence.

Option (1) is incorrect because it is a fragment—sentence 2 is a fragment that lacks a verb. Option (2) changes the verb tense of sentence 3, but it does not fix the sentence fragment in sentence 2. Option (3) combines the two ideas, but forms a comma splice, which is also incorrect. Option (4) does not fix the sentence fragment because a semicolon alone cannot be used to combine a fragment and an independent clause.

2. (3) death are not
Option (3) is correct because it supplies a verb (*are*) to make a complete sentence.

Option (1) is incorrect because it is a fragment that lacks a verb. Option (2) makes two sentences, but the first sentence is still a fragment. Option (4) makes two clauses but does not fix the fragment in the first clause. Option (5) creates a comma splice, or run-on sentence, which is also incorrect.

Sentence Fragments

Directions: Choose the one best answer to each question.

Questions 1 through 4 refer to the following paragraph.

(1) More and more Americans are telecommuting. (2) Telecommuting working from home instead of going to your employer's office. (3) This new method of working saves travel time and saves money on work clothes and gas. (4) Employees simply walk into their offices at home, wearing whatever is comfortable, and begin working at their own desks. (5) Companies allow telecommuting for various reasons. (6) Increased worker morale and decreased need for office space. (7) Because telecommuters need to be sure, however, that they consider all aspects of working at home.

1. Sentence 2: **Telecommuting working from home instead of going to your employer's office.**

   Which is the best way to write the underlined portion of this sentence? If the original is the best way, choose option (1).

   (1) Telecommuting working
   (2) Telecommuting, working
   (3) Telecommuting is working
   (4) Telecommuting and working
   (5) Telecommuting because working

> **TIP**
>
> Determine whether a group of words is a sentence fragment by reading it as if it were the only sentence in the paragraph. Does it make sense without any other information? Does it have a subject and a verb? Can it stand alone? If not, it is probably a sentence fragment.

---

2. Sentence 4: **Employees simply walk into their offices at home, wearing whatever is comfortable, and begin working at their own desks.**

   Which correction should be made to sentence 4?

   (1) remove comma after home
   (2) remove comma after comfortable
   (3) replace and with when
   (4) replace and with they
   (5) no correction is necessary

3. Sentences 5 and 6: **Companies allow telecommuting for various reasons. Increased worker morale and decreased need for office space.**

   The most effective combination of sentences 5 and 6 would include which group of words?

   (1) reasons, such as increased
   (2) reasons, because increased
   (3) reasons, increased
   (4) reasons; increased
   (5) reasons, although increased

4. Sentence 7: **Because telecommuters need to be sure, however, that they consider all aspects of working at home.**

   Which correction should be made to sentence 7?

   (1) replace Because telecommuters with Telecommuters
   (2) replace Because with Since
   (3) insert a comma after need
   (4) remove however
   (5) no correction is necessary

Questions 5 through 9 refer to the following paragraph.

(1) Technology now exists that allows us to determine precisely where anything is located on Earth. (2) Global positioning. (3) Orbiting satellites beam very precise data. (4) Special receivers on the earth's surface. (5) Although then the new technology lets people use a hand-held device to determine where they are. (6) With one of these devices, hikers or drivers would never get lost. (7) Objects, whether they are moving or stationary. (8) They could be located easily. (9) Any stolen car could be found quickly.

5. Sentence 2: **Global positioning.**

Which is the best way to write sentence 2? If the original is the best way, choose option (1).

(1) Global positioning.
(2) This technology is global positioning.
(3) Called global positioning.
(4) It is called, global positioning.
(5) Global positioning;

6. Sentences 3 and 4: **Orbiting satellites beam very precise data. Special receivers on the earth's surface.**

Which is the best way to write the underlined portion of these sentences? If the original is the best way, choose option (1).

(1) very precise data. Special receivers
(2) very precise data. Receivers
(3) very precise data to special receivers
(4) very precise receiver data
(5) very precise receivers to special data

7. Sentence 5: **Although then the new technology lets people use a hand-held device to determine exactly where they are.**

Which correction should be made to sentence 5?

(1) replace Although then with Then
(2) insert a comma after device
(3) replace lets with let's
(4) Insert at after are
(5) no correction is necessary

8. Sentence 6: **With one of these devices, hikers or drivers would never get lost.**

Which correction should be made to sentence 6?

(1) remove comma after devices
(2) insert a period after devices and capitalize hikers
(3) insert a comma after drivers
(4) replace hikers or drivers with receivers
(5) no correction is necessary

9. Sentences 7 and 8: **Objects, whether they are moving or stationary. They could be located easily.**

Which is the best way to write the underlined portion of these sentences? If the original is the best way, choose option (1).

(1) moving or stationary. They could be
(2) moving or stationary they could be
(3) moving, or stationary could be
(4) moving or stationary, could be
(5) moving or stationary; could be

Answers and explanations start on page 109.

Skill 2

Run-On Sentences

Run-on sentences are another common writing error. A run-on sentence contains **two or more sentences** without **punctuation** to separate them.

Run-on sentence: The night was beautiful it was cold.

You can correct run-on sentences several ways:

Method 1: Use a period to create separate sentences.
The night was <u>beautiful. It</u> was cold.

Method 2: Use a conjunction to join the two clauses into a single sentence.
The night was beautiful <u>and</u> cold.

Method 3: Join the two clauses with a comma and a coordinating conjunction.
The night was <u>beautiful, but</u> it was cold.

Method 4: Subordinate one clause to another.
<u>Although</u> the night was beautiful, it was cold.

Method 5: If the two clauses are closely related, join them with a semicolon.
The night was <u>beautiful; it</u> was cold.

Method 6: Join the two clauses with a semicolon, a conjunctive adverb, and a comma.
The night was <u>beautiful; however,</u> it was cold.

Read the sentence below. Choose the <u>one best answer</u> to the question.

Fuel costs have skyrocketed they are changing how people live.

QUESTION: Which correction should be made to this sentence?

(1) Fuel costs have skyrocketed, they are changing how people live.
(2) Fuel costs are changing how people live.
(3) Although fuel costs have skyrocketed, they are changing how people live.
(4) Fuel costs have skyrocketed; however they are changing how people live.
(5) Fuel costs have skyrocketed, and they are changing how people live.

EXPLANATIONS

(1) No. Adding only a comma isn't enough. The sentence is now a comma splice.
(2) No. Although this is a complete sentence, part of the writer's thought is missing.
(3) No. Subordinating the clause by adding the word *although* doesn't work here, because the meaning is illogical.
(4) No. The adverb *however* changes the meaning, implying an unnecessary contrast.
(5) **Yes. Adding a comma and a conjunction (*and*) repairs this run-on sentence.**

ANSWER: (5) Fuel costs have skyrocketed, and they are changing how people live.

Practice the Skill

Try these examples. Choose the <u>one best answer</u> to each question. Then check your answers and read the explanations.

(1) Sociologists say that a major change in American life has been the move from limited options to many choices. (2) Nowhere is this change more obvious than when we turn on our TV sets. (3) Our choices once consisted of three networks compare that to today's cable services. (4) People like having options, many of us wonder if we really need more than 100 channels.

1. Sentence 3: **Our choices once consisted of <u>three networks compare</u> that to today's cable services.**

   Which is the <u>best</u> way to write the underlined portion of this sentence? If the original option is the best way, choose option (1).

   (1) three networks compare
   (2) three networks and compare
   (3) three networks, and compare
   (4) three networks. Compare
   (5) three networks, however compare

   HINT Is this a run-on sentence? If so, find the two distinct ideas to see how closely they relate in order to choose the best way to write them.

2. Sentence 4: **People like having options, many of us wonder if we really need more than 100 channels.**

   Which correction should be made to sentence 4?

   (1) replace <u>People</u> with <u>Although people</u>
   (2) remove the comma after <u>options</u>
   (3) replace <u>options,</u> with <u>options; but</u>
   (4) change <u>options,</u> to <u>options and,</u>
   (5) no correction is necessary

   HINT How do the two ideas in this sentence relate to each other? Are they the same, or do they contrast? What is the best way to express them in a single sentence?

Answers and Explanations

1. (4) three networks. Compare
Option (4) is correct because it uses a period to create two distinct sentences.

The original (option 1) is incorrect because it is a run-on sentence. Although adding the conjunction *and* after *networks* (option 2) or adding a comma and the conjunction *and* in that position (option 3) does create a complete sentence, these options join ideas that would be better expressed separately. Adding a comma and *however* after *networks* (option 5) creates a comma splice and changes the meaning.

2. (1) replace <u>People</u> with <u>Although people</u>
Replacing *people* with *Although people* (option 1) corrects the sentence by subordinating the first thought to the second, creating a sentence that is complete and makes sense.

Removing the comma (option 2) does not correct the run-on. Option (3) is incorrect because you should not use a coordinating conjunction (*but*) with a semicolon. Option (4) incorrectly places an awkward conjunction before the comma, rather than after it. The original (option 5) is incorrect because it is a run-on sentence.

Run-On Sentences

Directions: Choose the one best answer to each question.

Questions 1 through 4 refer to the following paragraph.

(1) The tourist wrestling with the heavy suitcases is probably an overpacker. (2) Heavy bags can cause serious back injuries, they ruin an expensive vacation. (3) Some overpackers defend their choices by saying, "You never know what you might need!" (4) Remember times have changed, we live in a shrinking world, and camera batteries are available almost everywhere. (5) Also, don't pack a separate outfit for each day avoid it. (6) Choose a few basic garments that you can mix and match by alternating tops and shirts and then use accessories like scarves or ties to vary the look. (7) Finally, don't pack too many pairs of shoes. Shoes they are heavy and require too much suitcase space.

1. Sentence 2: **Heavy bags can cause serious back injuries, they ruin an expensive vacation.**

   Which is the best way to write the underlined portion of this sentence? If the original is the best way, choose option (1).

   (1) back injuries, they ruin
   (2) back injuries, ruining
   (3) back injuries; ruining
   (4) back injuries; like ruining
   (5) back injuries, although ruining

> **TIP**
>
> Not every long sentence is a run-on. Some sentences may technically be grammatically correct, but they can have too much information for a reader to process easily. Trust your eyes and ears to help you decide how to revise such sentences.

2. Sentence 3: **Some overpackers defend their choices by saying, "You never know what you might need!"**

   Which correction should be made to sentence 3?

   (1) break into two sentences after choices
   (2) replace the comma after saying with a semicolon
   (3) insert a comma after choices
   (4) change by saying to to say
   (5) no correction is necessary

3. Sentence 5: **Also, don't pack a separate outfit for each day avoid it.**

   Which is the best way to rewrite the sentence?

   (1) Don't pack a separate outfit for each day avoid it.
   (2) Avoid don't pack a separate outfit for each day.
   (3) Also, pack a separate outfit for each day.
   (4) Also, avoid packing a separate outfit for each day.
   (5) Avoid, also don't pack a separate outfit for each day.

4. Sentence 6: **Choose a few basic garments that you can mix and match by alternating tops and shirts and then use accessories like scarves or ties to vary the look.**

   Which is the best way to write the underlined portion of this sentence? If the original is the best way, choose option (1).

   (1) tops and shirts and then use
   (2) tops and shirts. Then use
   (3) tops and shirts, then use
   (4) tops and shirts but then use
   (5) tops and shirts; besides, you can then use

Questions 5 through 9 refer to the following paragraph.

(1) We all know that dictionaries contain definitions. (2) If you don't know what *salubrious* means or how to pronounce *scherzo* reaching for a dictionary. (3) However, a dictionary contains more than a lot of words it is a reference book as well. (4) My dictionary contains the entire text of the Declaration of Independence, the Constitution, and all of its amendments. (5) I can also find a list of the highest mountains in the world, although however I am not planning to climb all of them. (6) Dictionaries they are a great reference for students even include the names of famous people and fictional characters.

5. Sentence 2: **If you don't know what *salubrious* means or how to <u>pronounce *scherzo* reaching</u> for a dictionary.**

Which is the <u>best</u> way to write the underlined portion of this sentence? If the original is the best way, choose option (1).

(1) pronounce *scherzo* reaching
(2) pronounce *scherzo*. Reaching
(3) pronounce *scherzo*, reach
(4) pronounce *scherzo* while reaching
(5) pronounce *scherzo*; reaching

6. Sentence 3: **However, a dictionary contains more than <u>a lot of words it is</u> a reference book as well.**

Which is the <u>best</u> way to write the underlined portion of this sentence? If the original is the best way, choose option (1).

(1) a lot of words it is
(2) a lot of words is
(3) a lot of words, it is
(4) a lot of words. It is
(5) a lot of words that is

7. Sentence 4: **My dictionary contains the entire text of the Declaration of Independence, the Constitution, and all of its amendments.**

Which correction should be made to sentence 4?

(1) insert period after <u>Independence</u>
(2) insert a comma after <u>text</u>
(3) remove the comma after <u>Independence</u>
(4) change <u>and</u> to <u>although</u>
(5) no correction is necessary

8. Sentence 5: **I can also find a list of the highest mountains in the <u>world, although</u> <u>however</u> I am not planning to climb all of them.**

Which is the <u>best</u> way to write the underlined portion of this sentence? If the original is the best way, choose option (1).

(1) world, although however
(2) world, although
(3) world although, however
(4) world and
(5) no correction is necessary

9. Sentence 6: **Dictionaries they are a great reference for students even include the names of famous people and fictional characters.**

If you rewrote sentence 6 beginning with <u>A great reference for</u> the next words would be

(1) dictionaries, students
(2) students, dictionaries even
(3) students' dictionaries
(4) names of famous people
(5) dictionaries, even including

Answers and explanations start on page 109.

Comma Splices

Another common error that you may see on the GED Writing Test is a **comma splice**. A comma splice occurs when two **independent clauses** (complete thoughts) are joined with just a **comma**.

Comma splice: Our car broke down, we were stranded in the middle of nowhere.

You can correct comma splices in several ways.

Method 1: Make two sentences. Separate the clauses with a period.

Our car broke <u>down. We</u> were stranded in the middle of nowhere.

Method 2: Join the two clauses with a comma and a **coordinating conjunction**. The coordinating conjunctions are *and, but, for, nor, or, so,* and *yet.* Make sure that the correction makes sense.

Our car broke <u>down, so</u> we were stranded in the middle of nowhere.

Method 3: Relate one clause to another by using a **subordinating conjunction**. Subordinating conjunctions include words such as *although, because, before, unless, until, when, whether,* and *while.* Choose one that makes sense.

<u>When</u> our car broke down, we were stranded in the middle of nowhere.

Method 4: If the ideas in the clauses are closely related, join them with a semicolon. You can also use a semicolon, a **conjunctive adverb**, and a comma. Conjunctive adverbs include *besides, consequently, however, indeed, meanwhile, moreover,* and *therefore.* Be sure the conjunctive adverb that you choose makes sense.

Our car broke <u>down; consequently,</u> we were stranded in the middle of nowhere.

Read the sentence below. Choose the <u>one best answer</u> to the question.

Workers who type a lot make repetitive motions that stress their hands and wrists, they may suffer carpal tunnel syndrome.

QUESTION: Which correction should be made to this sentence?

    (1) remove the comma
    (2) replace <u>Workers</u> with <u>Because workers</u>
    (3) insert <u>nor</u> after the comma
    (4) make two sentences by inserting a period after <u>motions</u>
    (5) no correction is necessary

EXPLANATIONS

    (1) No. Removing the comma creates a run-on sentence.
    (2) Yes. Adding *Because* correctly subordinates the first clause and relates the ideas.
    (3) No. The sentence does not make sense with this coordinating conjunction.
    (4) No. This option leaves a comma splice in the second sentence.
    (5) No. The sentence is a comma splice that needs to be corrected.

ANSWER: (2) replace <u>Workers</u> with <u>Because workers</u>

Practice the Skill

Try these sample questions. Choose the one best answer to each question. Then check your answers and read the explanations.

(1) An ordinary kitchen timer can be used in an unexpected way. (2) Some couples use this simple household item as a timekeeper, it may be used when there is a disagreement. (3) One person takes three minutes to state his or her view of the problem, the other person gets an equal turn. (4) This practice helps to keep a simple difference of opinion from turning into a nasty argument.

1. Sentence 2: **Some couples use this simple household item as a <u>timekeeper, it may be used when</u> there is a disagreement.**

Which is the <u>best</u> way to write the underlined portion of this sentence? If the original is the best way, choose option (1).

(1) timekeeper, it may be used when
(2) timekeeper it may be used when
(3) timekeeper. It may be used when
(4) timekeeper, but it may be used when
(5) timekeeper, yet it may be used when

HINT Does the sentence use a comma to join two complete thoughts? If so, which answer choice corrects the error?

2. Sentence 3: **One person takes three minutes to state his or her view of the <u>problem, the other person</u> gets an equal turn.**

Which correction should be made to sentence 3?

(1) problem the other person
(2) problem, and the other person
(3) problem, but the other person
(4) problem, nor the other person
(5) no correction is necessary

HINT How can you tell whether this sentence is a comma splice? If it is a comma splice, which option corrects the error and makes the most sense?

Answers and Explanations

1. (3) timekeeper. It may be used when
Option (3) is correct because it repairs the comma splice by adding a period to create two complete sentences.

The original (option 1) is incorrect because it is a comma splice of two independent clauses. Option (2) is incorrect because it creates a run-on sentence in which the two independent clauses are joined without punctuation to separate them. While inserting *but* (option 4) or *yet* (option 5) repairs the comma splice, these options are incorrect because the sentences do not make sense.

2. (2) problem, and the other person
Option (2) is correct because it adds the conjunction *and* to create a sentence that fixes the comma splice of two independent clauses and makes sense.

Option (1) is incorrect because it creates a run-on sentence in which the two independent clauses are joined without punctuation to separate them. While options (3) and (4) use coordinating conjunctions properly to repair the comma splice by joining the two independent clauses, these options are incorrect because they create sentences that do not make sense. Option (5) is wrong because there is a comma splice that needs to be fixed.

Comma Splices

Directions: Choose the one best answer to each question.

Questions 1 through 5 refer to the following paragraph.

(1) Sailplane soaring is the safest of the aerial sports, it is as thrilling as more dangerous ones. (2) Using rising warm-air currents rather than engine power, a sailplane pilot can gain stupendous altitude. (3) Experienced fliers can keep a sailplane aloft all day, they can cover hundreds of miles. (4) The sensation of flight in a plane that is not powered by engines is quite unique. (5) The flier is suspended in midair, experiencing little vibration and no noise, he feels the rush of the wind. (6) Pilots say they experience an exhilarating sense of freedom, they also experience a profound calm.

1. Sentence 1: **Sailplane soaring is the safest of the aerial sports, it is as thrilling as more dangerous ones.**

   Which correction should be made to sentence 1?

   (1) replace Sailplane with When sailplane
   (2) insert or after the comma
   (3) insert but after the comma
   (4) remove the comma
   (5) no correction is necessary

2. Sentence 2: **Using rising warm-air currents rather than engine power, a sailplane pilot can gain stupendous altitude.**

   Which correction should be made to sentence 2?

   (1) change Using to Use
   (2) insert a comma after currents
   (3) insert and after the comma
   (4) remove the comma
   (5) no correction is necessary

3. Sentence 3: **Experienced fliers can keep a sailplane aloft all day, they can cover hundreds of miles.**

   Which is the best way to write the underlined portion of this sentence? If the original is the best way, choose option (1).

   (1) day, they can cover
   (2) day they can cover
   (3) day, but they can cover
   (4) day, and they can cover
   (5) day, when they can cover

4. Sentence 5: **The flier is suspended in midair, experiencing little vibration and no noise, he feels the rush of the wind.**

   Which is the best way to write the underlined portion of this sentence? If the original is the best way, choose option (1).

   (1) noise, he feels
   (2) noise there is
   (3) noise or there is
   (4) noise, although he feels
   (5) noise. Though he feels

5. Sentence 6: **Pilots say they experience an exhilarating sense of freedom, they also experience a profound calm.**

   Which is the best way to write the underlined portion of this sentence? If the original is the best way, choose option (1).

   (1) freedom, they also experience
   (2) freedom. They also experience
   (3) freedom, however they also experience
   (4) freedom they also experience
   (5) freedom whenever they also experience

Questions 6 through 9 refer to the following paragraph.

(1) Parents who are expecting a baby should start keeping medical records even before the baby is born. (2) Practically, these records are like a personal diary, the parents should record all medical events, even before the baby's birth. (3) A child's records should begin with any prenatal problems or complications in the hospital after birth. (4) After the child is born, parents should list immunizations, doctor appointments, and illnesses. (5) The history should include prescription and non-prescription medications, it should note any negative reactions to medications. (6) Parents maintaining useful records, they can supply invaluable information to medical professionals.

6. Sentence 2: **Practically, these records are like a personal <u>diary, the parents</u> should record all medical events, even before the baby's birth.**

Which is the <u>best</u> way to write the underlined portion of this sentence? If the original is the best way, choose option (1).

(1) diary, the parents
(2) diary the parents
(3) diary; the parents
(4) diary, but the parents
(5) diary, or the parents

7. Sentence 3: **A child's records should begin with any prenatal problems or complications in the hospital after birth.**

Which correction should be made to sentence 3?

(1) insert a period after <u>problems</u>
(2) insert a comma after <u>problems</u>
(3) insert <u>although</u> after <u>problems</u>
(4) insert a comma after <u>prenatal</u>
(5) no correction is necessary

8. Sentence 5: **The history should include prescription and non-prescription <u>medications, it should note</u> any negative reactions to medications.**

Which is the <u>best</u> way to write the underlined portion of this sentence? If the original is the best way, choose option (1).

(1) medications, it should note
(2) medications it should note
(3) medications, and it should note
(4) medications, however it should note
(5) medications. Should it note

9. Sentence 6: **Parents maintaining useful records, they can supply invaluable information to medical professionals.**

Which is the most effective way to rewrite sentence 6?

(1) By maintaining useful records, parents can supply invaluable information to medical professionals.
(2) Parents maintaining useful records, however, they can supply invaluable information to medical professionals.
(3) Parents maintaining useful records can be invaluable. Suppliers of information to medical professionals.
(4) Parents, who maintaining useful records can supply, invaluable information to medical professionals.
(5) no revision is necessary

Answers and explanations start on page 110.

> [**TIP**]
>
> To decide whether a sentence contains a comma splice, check whether the words on either side of the comma could stand alone as complete sentences. If they can, use one of the methods described on page 18 to correct the comma splice.

KEY Skill 4

Combining Sentences

Combining **short sentences** can improve the style and clarity of writing. There are several ways to **combine sentences** to make them clearer, smoother, and more effective.

Method 1: Combine sentences with a **comma** and a **coordinating conjunction** such as *and, but, for, nor, or, yet,* and *so.*
She looked for an apartment. She couldn't find one.
She looked for an apartment, <u>but</u> she couldn't find one.

Method 2: Combine sentences by using a **subordinating conjunction** and a **comma**, and subordinating one sentence to another.
He wanted a new car. He couldn't afford one.
<u>Although</u> he wanted a new car, he couldn't afford one.

Method 3: Combine sentences by turning one of the sentences into a **prepositional phrase.**
The dog trotted rapidly. The dog wore a red collar.
The dog <u>with the red collar</u> trotted rapidly.

Method 4: Combine closely related sentences with a **semicolon**.
She went to work. She did her job.
She went to work<u>;</u> she did her job.

Method 5: Combine sentences with a **conjunctive adverb** and a semicolon. Be sure to use an adverb that makes sense in the context of the sentence.
William spoke as loudly as he could. His audience still couldn't hear.
William spoke as loudly as he could<u>; however</u>, his audience still couldn't hear.

Read the sentences below. Choose the <u>one best answer</u> to the question.

Martha always had an interest in animals. Her interest led her to her career.

QUESTION: Which combination of these sentences is most effective?

(1) Martha always had an interest in animals, and it led her to her career.
(2) Martha always had an interest in animals, although it led her to her career.
(3) Martha, always interested in animals, led her to her career.
(4) Martha always in her career had an interest in animals.
(5) Martha always had an interest; animals led to her career.

EXPLANATIONS

(1) **Yes. Correctly using the conjunction *and* relates and connects the sentences.**
(2) No. This choice is incorrect because *although* does not make sense in the sentence.
(3) No. The sentence is incorrect because Martha did not lead herself.
(4) No. This combination incorrectly changes the information in the two sentences.
(5) No. This choice is incorrect because animals did not lead to Martha's career.

ANSWER: (1) Martha always had an interest in animals, and it led her to her career.

Practice the Skill

Try these sample questions. Choose the one best answer to each question. Then check your answers and read the explanations.

(1) Your flight to Chicago will take six hours. (2) You may want to bring reading material or work to pass the time. (3) When you arrive, Elaine Williams will meet you at the airport. (4) Elaine works at the Michigan Avenue office. (5) The Michigan Avenue office is located downtown. (6) The drive from the airport to downtown is minimal. (7) You should arrive for the meeting on time.

1. Sentences 1 and 2: **Your flight to Chicago will take six hours. You may want to bring reading material or work to pass the time.**

The most effective combination of sentences 1 and 2 would include which group of words?

(1) hours, you
(2) hours, but you
(3) hours, so you
(4) hours, therefore you
(5) hours; finally you

HINT Which choice combines the ideas of the two sentences most smoothly? Choose new punctuation carefully to avoid creating new errors such as comma splices or run-on sentences.

2. Sentences 3 and 4: **When you arrive, Elaine Williams will meet you at the airport. Elaine works at the Michigan Avenue office.**

The most effective combination of sentences 3 and 4 would include which group of words?

(1) airport then she works
(2) airport; therefore Elaine
(3) airport, she works
(4) Elaine Williams, finally at
(5) Elaine Williams, from the

HINT Which choice puts the most information in the sentence in the simplest way? Be certain that the new sentence retains all necessary information from both original sentences.

Answers and Explanations

1. (3) hours, so you
Option (3) is correct because it combines the sentences smoothly with a comma and the coordinating conjunction *so*, which links and relates the sentences' ideas.

Option (1) is incorrect because it creates a comma splice, as does option (4). The word *but* in option (2) incorrectly changes the meaning of the sentences. Option (5) is incorrect because the word *finally* changes the meaning of the sentences, although the semicolon is placed properly.

2. (5) Elaine Williams, from the
Option (5) correctly inserts a prepositional phrase *from the Michigan Avenue office* to combine the sentences in the simplest and clearest way.

Option (1) is incorrect because it creates a run-on sentence. Option (2) is incorrect because *therefore* changes the meaning of the sentences. Option (3) is incorrect because it creates a comma splice. Option (4) incorrectly changes the meaning of the sentences with *finally*.

Combining Sentences

Directions: Choose the one best answer to each question.

Questions 1 through 5 refer to the following paragraph.

(1) The average American uses 123 gallons of water daily. (2) A family of four uses 492 gallons a day. (3) These figures seem enormous. (4) They are easier to understand when you consider what they include. (5) Taking a shower uses about 20 gallons alone. (6) Washing dishes by hand uses about 20 gallons. (7) Running a dishwasher load uses only about 10 gallons. (8) Surprisingly, even brushing your teeth uses about one gallon. (9) You use a gallon of water with each brushing. (10) In the future, clean water will be ever more important. (11) We should conserve water.

1. Sentences 1 and 2: **The average American uses 123 gallons of water daily. A family of four uses 492 gallons a day.**

   The most effective combination of sentences 1 and 2 would include which group of words?

   (1) water daily, a family
   (2) water daily; instead a family
   (3) water daily, however a family
   (4) water daily; therefore, a family
   (5) water daily a family

2. Sentences 3 and 4: **These figures seem enormous. They are easier to understand when you consider what they include.**

   Which is the best way to write the underlined portion of these sentences? If the original is the best way, choose option (1).

   (1) enormous. They
   (2) enormous, whenever they
   (3) enormous; thus they
   (4) enormous, but they
   (5) enormous, when they

3. Sentences 6 and 7: **Washing dishes by hand uses about 20 gallons. Running a dishwasher load uses only about 10 gallons.**

   The most effective combination of sentences 6 and 7 would include which group of words?

   (1) gallons, so running
   (2) gallons; however, running
   (3) gallons; likewise running
   (4) gallons, for running
   (5) gallons; besides,

4. Sentences 8 and 9: **Surprisingly, even brushing your teeth uses about one gallon. You use a gallon of water with each brushing.**

   The most effective combination of sentences 8 and 9 would include which group of words?

   (1) gallon, and you use
   (2) gallon, using a gallon
   (3) gallon; because you use
   (4) gallon with each brushing.
   (5) gallon; you use a gallon

5. Sentences 10 and 11: **In the future, clean water will be ever more important. We should conserve water.**

   Which combination of these sentences is most effective?

   (1) Clean water will be ever more important in the future, we should conserve water.
   (2) Clean water will be ever more important in the future, so we should conserve it.
   (3) Clean water will be ever more important in the future, although we should conserve it.
   (4) Clean water will be ever more important so we should conserve the future.
   (5) Clean water will be ever more important in the future; next we should conserve it.

Questions 6 through 10 refer to the following paragraph.

(1) Most people think a cooked lobster has been boiled. (2) It shouldn't be immersed in water. (3) Boiling a lobster ensures that it will be thoroughly cooked. (4) It will be soggy. (5) A lobster should be cooked in a small amount of water. (6) It will steam and have a full flavor. (7) Only about two inches of salted water should cover the bottom of the lobster pot. (8) When the water boils, add the lobster. (9) In about 20 minutes, the lobster will be well steamed. (10) Before you begin eating, don't forget to put on your bib!

6. Sentences 1 and 2: **Most people think a cooked lobster has been boiled. It shouldn't be immersed in water.**

The most effective combination of sentences 1 and 2 would include which group of words?

(1) boiled, it shouldn't
(2) boiled, so it shouldn't
(3) boiled, because it shouldn't
(4) boiled; however, it shouldn't
(5) boiled, and it shouldn't

7. Sentences 3 and 4: **Boiling a lobster ensures that it will be thoroughly <u>cooked. It</u> will be soggy.**

Which is the <u>best</u> way to write the underlined portion of these sentences? If the original is the best way, choose option (1).

(1) cooked. It
(2) cooked; it
(3) cooked, but it
(4) cooked, moreover it
(5) cooked, it

8. Sentences 5 and 6: **A lobster should be cooked in a small amount of water. It will steam and have a full flavor.**

The most effective combination of sentences 5 and 6 would include which group of words?

(1) water, so it will
(2) water in the steam and full flavor
(3) water; however it will
(4) water, finally it will
(5) water, but it will

9. Sentences 7 and 8: **Only about two inches of salted water should cover the bottom of the lobster pot. When the water boils, add the lobster.**

The most effective combination of sentences 7 and 8 would include which group of words?

(1) pot; therefore
(2) pot, but when
(3) pot; similarly
(4) pot, and when
(5) pot, add

10. Sentences 9 and 10: **In about 20 minutes, the lobster will be well steamed. Before you begin eating, don't forget to put on your bib!**

The most effect combination of sentences 9 and 10 would include which group of words? If the original is the best way, choose option (1).

(1) well steamed. Before you
(2) well. Steamed before you
(3) well steamed before you
(4) well steamed, before you
(5) well steamed, however

> **TIP**
>
> Before you combine sentences, decide what relationship exists between the ideas in the sentences. Then you can be sure to combine the sentences in a way that keeps the ideas related.

Answers and explanations start on page 111.

Skill 5

Parallel Structure

Parallel structure means that equal and **related words** and **phrases** must use the same grammatical form.

Verbs, nouns, adjectives, or adverbs **in a series** must use the same grammatical form.

Parallel Structure: She is happy, charming, and beautiful.
Non-Parallel Structure: She is happy, charming, and has beauty. (*Has beauty* is not parallel to the adjectives *happy* and *charming*.)

Parallel Structure: The ad shows the desk's size, color, and price.
Non-Parallel Structure: The ad shows the desk's size, color, and how much it costs. (*How much it costs* is not parallel to the nouns *size* and *color*.)

Words and phrases in a series also must use the same grammatical form.

Parallel Structure: She grows vegetables for exercise, necessity, and pleasure.
Non-Parallel Structure: She grows vegetables for exercise, necessity, and to gain pleasure. (*To gain pleasure* is not parallel to the nouns *exercise* and *necessity*.)

Read the sentence below. Choose the <u>one best answer</u> to the question.

At the gym, I enjoy rope-jumping, lifting weights, and the stationary bike.

QUESTION: Which correction should be made to this sentence?

   (1) replace <u>enjoy rope-jumping</u> with <u>jumped rope</u>
   (2) replace <u>lifting weights</u> with <u>weight-lifted</u>
   (3) replace <u>stationary bike</u> with <u>rode the stationary bike</u>
   (4) replace <u>and the stationary bike</u> with <u>and using the stationary bike</u>
   (5) no correction is necessary

EXPLANATIONS

   (1) No. This option is incorrect because <u>jumped rope</u> is not parallel to any other elements in the series.
   (2) No. This option is incorrect because <u>weight-lifted</u> is not parallel to any other elements, and does not make sense with the verb *enjoy*.
   (3) No. This option is incorrect because <u>rode the stationary bike</u> is not parallel to the first two verb phrases.
   (4) **Yes. <u>And using the stationary bike</u> is a verb phrase that is parallel to <u>rope-jumping</u> and <u>lifting weights</u>.**
   (5) No. This choice is incorrect because the third item in the series is not parallel.

ANSWER: (4) replace <u>and the stationary bike</u> with <u>and using the stationary bike</u>

Practice the Skill

(1) Each workday we must check figures, talk to clients, and make decisions about supplies to order. (2) Unfortunately, we are distracted by the phone, e-mail, and our boss calling meetings. (3) We must balance all of these parts of our workday to do our jobs effectively. (4) Many experts recommend that employees plan their days in advance to better manage time. (5) Prioritize your tasks for the day and decide which are the most important to complete by day's end. (6) Minimize distractions by following a set schedule. (7) Creating and sticking to a schedule will dramatically improve your productivity and work flow.

1. Sentence 1: **Each workday we must check figures, talk to clients, and make decisions about products to order.**

   Which correction should be made to sentence 1?

   (1) change <u>check</u> to <u>checking</u>
   (2) change <u>talk</u> to <u>talked</u>
   (3) change <u>make decisions</u> to <u>deciding</u>
   (4) change <u>order</u> to <u>ordered</u>
   (5) no correction is necessary

   HINT Find the items that are in a series. Do they use the same grammatical form?

2. Sentence 2: **Unfortunately, we are distracted by the phone, e-mail, and our boss calling meetings.**

   Which correction should be made to sentence 2?

   (1) replace <u>the phone</u> with <u>make phone calls</u>
   (2) replace <u>e-mail</u> with <u>receiving e-mail</u>
   (3) replace <u>our boss</u> with <u>the boss</u>
   (4) replace <u>our boss calling meetings</u> with <u>meetings called by our boss</u>
   (5) no correction is necessary

   HINT Look carefully at the nouns in the series. Are they all related and do they use the same grammatical form?

Answers and Explanations

1. (5) no correction is necessary
Option (5), the original sentence, is correct. <u>Check figures</u>, <u>talk to clients</u>, and <u>make decisions</u> are parallel verb phrases.

Options (1), (2), (3), and (4) change verb forms in ways that create non-parallel structures.

2. (4) replace <u>our boss calling meetings</u> with <u>meetings called by our boss</u>
Option (4) correctly adds <u>meetings</u> to the list of distractions, which already includes the parallel nouns <u>phone</u> and <u>e-mail</u>.

Options (1) and (2) are incorrect because <u>make phone calls</u> and <u>receiving e-mail</u> are verb phrases, which are not the same grammatical form as the nouns already in the series. Option (3) does not correct the non-parallel structure of the series items. The original sentence, (option 5), contains a non-parallel structure.

Parallel Structure

Directions: Choose the <u>one best answer</u> to each question.

<u>Questions 1 through 5</u> refer to the following paragraph.

(1) The tall Afghan hound is an ancient, respected, and most people think attractive dog breed. (2) The Afghan has a curling tail, is long-eared, and has long legs. (3) The Afghan also has thick, long, flowing hair. (4) Afghans are aloof, stubborn, and have a sweet disposition. (5) For such a large and stately dog, the Afghan is surprisingly affectionate. (6) Afghans like to hunt, to run, and being by themselves outside.

1. Sentence 1: **The tall Afghan hound is an ancient, respected, and most people think attractive dog breed.**

   Which correction should be made to sentence 1?

   (1) remove <u>most people think</u>
   (2) remove <u>an</u>
   (3) insert <u>a</u> before <u>respected</u>
   (4) insert <u>an</u> before <u>attractive</u>
   (5) no correction is necessary

2. Sentence 2: **The Afghan has a curling tail, is long-eared, and has long legs.**

   If you rewrote sentence 2 beginning with <u>With a curling tail, long ears, and</u> the next words should be

   (1) having long legs
   (2) has long legs
   (3) legs that are long,
   (4) runs on long legs
   (5) long legs,

3. Sentence 3: **The Afghan also has thick, long, flowing hair.**

   Which correction should be made to sentence 3?

   (1) change <u>flowing</u> to <u>flow</u>
   (2) replace <u>thick, long, flowing hair</u> with <u>thick hair, long hair, flowing hair</u>
   (3) remove the commas
   (4) insert <u>has</u> before <u>long</u>
   (5) no correction is necessary

4. Sentence 4: **Afghans are aloof, stubborn, and have a sweet disposition.**

   If you rewrote sentence 4 beginning with <u>Afghans are aloof, stubborn, and</u> the next word or words should be

   (1) have a sweet disposition
   (2) sweet
   (3) sweetly
   (4) are sweet dispositioned
   (5) with a sweet disposition

5. Sentence 6: **Afghans like to hunt, to run, and <u>being by themselves</u> outside.**

   Which is the <u>best</u> way to write the underlined portion of this sentence? If the original is the best way, choose option (1).

   (1) being by themselves
   (2) to be by themselves
   (3) want to be by themselves
   (4) are glad to be by themselves
   (5) be by themselves

Questions 6 through 9 refer to the following paragraph.

(1) In October, the states of Vermont and Maine have spectacular colors, crisp weather, and leaves that fall. (2) Although they are green in spring, the leaves turn bright red, rich orange, and yellow that shines in autumn. (3) The water in the lakes is blue, clear, and it sparkles. (4) For many years, tourists have traveled long distances to see these sights. (5) Maine and Vermont have become favorite destinations for hikers, bicyclists, and people who take pictures. (6) Visitors always enjoy the fresh country air and the beautiful colors of the New England landscape.

6. Sentence 1: **In October, the states of Vermont and Maine have spectacular colors, crisp weather, and leaves that fall.**

Which is the best way to write the underlined portion of this sentence? If the original is the best way, choose option (1).

(1) leaves that fall.
(2) leaves who fall.
(3) leaves are falling.
(4) falling leaves.
(5) leaves fall.

7. Sentence 2: **Although they are green in spring, the leaves turn bright red, rich orange, and yellow that shines in autumn.**

Which correction should be made to sentence 2?

(1) insert turn before rich
(2) insert turn before rich and before yellow
(3) insert that shines after red and after orange
(4) change yellow that shines to shining yellow
(5) remove in autumn

8. Sentence 3: **The water in the lakes is blue, clear, and it sparkles.**

Which correction should be made to sentence 3?

(1) insert is before clear
(2) insert it before clear
(3) change it sparkles to sparkling
(4) change it sparkles to which sparkles
(5) no correction is necessary

9. Sentence 5: **Maine and Vermont have become favorite destinations for hikers, bicyclists, and people who take pictures.**

Which is the best way to write the underlined portion of this sentence? If the original is the best way, choose option (1).

(1) and people who take pictures.
(2) and photographers.
(3) photographers.
(4) people taking pictures.
(5) and taking pictures.

TIP

Sentences that have a series sometimes cause problems with parallel structure. Check a series especially carefully to see that the grammatical forms match each other.

Answers and explanations start on page 111.

Usage

Verb Tenses

On the GED Writing Test, you may see questions about **verb tenses**. Verb tenses tell when an action takes place or when a condition exists. The verb tense used in a sentence must make sense for the idea being expressed. It must also make sense for the ideas expressed in surrounding sentences. There are three different kinds of verb tenses: **simple, continuing,** and **perfect**.

Simple tenses show actions that take place in the present, past, or future.

> **Present:** I <u>work</u> 40 hours each week.
> **Past:** However, last week I <u>worked</u> 45 hours.
> **Future:** Next week, I <u>will work</u> only 37 hours.

Continuing tenses show actions that are ongoing for an indefinite period in either the present, past, or future.

> **Present Continuous:** I <u>am working</u> with my dad now.
> **Past Continuous:** Last year, I <u>was working</u> at the hardware store.
> **Future Continuous:** I <u>will be working</u> for myself next year.

Perfect tenses show actions completed in either the present, past, or future.

> **Present Perfect:** I <u>have worked</u> 40 hours this week.
> **Past Perfect:** I <u>had worked</u> lots of overtime last month.
> **Future Perfect:** I <u>will have worked</u> 85 hours by the end of next week.

Read the sentence below. Choose the <u>one best answer</u> to the question.

Next month, I worked Tuesday through Sunday every week.

QUESTION: Which correction should be made to this sentence?

(1) change <u>worked</u> to <u>work</u>
(2) change <u>worked</u> to <u>was working</u>
(3) change <u>worked</u> to <u>had worked</u>
(4) change <u>worked</u> to <u>have worked</u>
(5) change <u>worked</u> to <u>will work</u>

EXPLANATIONS

(1) No. *Next month* shows that the action will take place in the future. The tense *work* puts the action in the present.
(2) No. *Next month* shows that the action will take place in the future. The tense *was working* puts the action in the past.
(3) No. *Next month* shows that the action will take place in the future. The tense *had worked* puts the action in the past.
(4) No. *Next month* shows that the action will take place in the future. The tense *have worked* puts the action in the past.
(5) **Yes. *Next month* tells us that the action will take place in the future. *Will work* is the correct form for a simple future tense verb.**

ANSWER: (5) change <u>worked</u> to <u>will work</u>

Practice the Skill

Try these examples. Choose the <u>one best answer</u> to each question. Then check your answers and read the explanations.

(1) Last week, my supervisor will ask me about overtime work. (2) As of today, I thought that I would like at least five extra hours per week. (3) I expect she will say that is no problem. (4) It's nice to work overtime because I get paid time and a half. (5) It's more money than I would earn in a normal week, and that money is a big help with the weekly bills and expenses. (6) If I can work five extra hours a week, I may be able to pay off my credit card earlier than expected, or I may be able to afford a greater downpayment on a new car. (7) A greater downpayment will mean a lower monthly payment.

1. Sentence 1: **Last week, my supervisor will ask me about overtime work.**

   Which correction should be made to sentence 1?

   (1) change <u>will ask</u> to <u>will have asked</u>
   (2) change <u>will ask</u> to <u>ask</u>
   (3) change <u>will ask</u> to <u>asked</u>
   (4) change <u>will ask</u> to <u>will be asking</u>
   (5) change <u>will ask</u> to <u>am asking</u>

   HINT Look for words other than verbs in the sentence that tell when the action takes place.

2. Sentence 2: **As of today, I <u>thought</u> that I would like at least five extra hours per week.**

   Which is the <u>best</u> way to write the underlined portion of this sentence? If the original is the best way, choose option (1).

   (1) thought
   (2) think
   (3) had thought
   (4) will think
   (5) will have thought

   HINT Check surrounding sentences to see what ideas are expressed. Make sure that the verb tense makes sense for those ideas.

Answers and Explanations

1. (3) change <u>will ask</u> to <u>asked</u>
Option (3) correctly uses a simple past tense verb for an action that happened in the past, as indicated by *Last week.*

Option (1) incorrectly uses the future perfect verb *will have asked*, but *Last week* indicates that the action took place in the past. Option (2) incorrectly uses a simple present tense verb, *ask*, but a past tense verb is needed. Option (4) uses a future continuous verb, *will be asking*, but a past tense verb is needed. Option (5) uses a present continuous verb, *will be asking*, but a past tense verb is needed.

2. (2) think
Option (2) correctly uses a simple present tense verb for an action happening in the present, as indicated by *As of today.*

Option (1) incorrectly uses the simple past tense verb *thought*, but *As of today* indicates that the action is taking place in the present. Option (3) incorrectly uses a past perfect verb, *had thought*, but a present tense verb is needed. Options (4) and (5) incorrectly use future tense verbs (the simple future tense verb *will think* and future perfect verb *will have thought*), but a present tense verb is needed.

Verb Tenses

Directions: Choose the one best answer to each question.

Questions 1 through 5 refer to the following paragraph.

(1) Today many people enjoy running marathons. (2) However, many runners may not know why we had called these races "marathons." (3) They are named for the plain of Marathon on the Greek peninsula, where many men are fighting a battle in 490 B.C. (4) The Greek army defeated the Persian army there. (5) According to legend, after the battle, the Greeks sent a messenger to Athens, about 25 miles away. (6) This runner delivered news of the victory; then he collapses and died. (7) Since 1896, the Olympic Games were honoring the runner's endurance by holding a race called the marathon.

1. Sentence 2: **However, many runners may not know why we had called the races "marathons."**

   Which correction should be made to sentence 2?

   (1) change <u>had called</u> to <u>will call</u>
   (2) change <u>had called</u> to <u>will have called</u>
   (3) change <u>had called</u> to <u>call</u>
   (4) change <u>had called</u> to <u>will be calling</u>
   (5) change <u>had called</u> to <u>were calling</u>

2. Sentence 3: **They are named for the plain of Marathon on the Greek peninsula, where many men are fighting a battle in 490 B.C.**

   Which is the <u>best</u> way to write the underlined portion of this sentence? If the original is the best way, choose option (1).

   (1) are fighting
   (2) fought
   (3) fight
   (4) will be fighting
   (5) have fought

3. Sentence 5: **According to legend, after the battle, the Greeks sent a messenger to Athens, about 25 miles away.**

   Which correction should be made to sentence 5?

   (1) change <u>sent</u> to <u>are sending</u>
   (2) change <u>sent</u> to <u>will be sent</u>
   (3) change <u>sent</u> to <u>send</u>
   (4) change <u>sent</u> to <u>were sending</u>
   (5) no correction is necessary

4. Sentence 6: **This runner <u>delivered news of the victory; then he collapses</u> and died.**

   Which is the <u>best</u> way to write the underlined portion of this sentence? If the original is the best way, choose option (1).

   (1) delivered news of the victory; then he collapses
   (2) was delivering news of the victory; then he collapses
   (3) delivered news of the victory; then he will have collapsed
   (4) delivered news of the victory; then he collapsed
   (5) had delivered news of the victory; then he collapses

5. Sentence 7: **Since 1896, the Olympic Games were honoring the runner's endurance by holding a race called the marathon.**

   Which correction should be made to sentence 7?

   (1) change <u>were honoring</u> to <u>have honored</u>
   (2) change <u>were honoring</u> to <u>are honoring</u>
   (3) change <u>were honoring</u> to <u>will be honoring</u>
   (4) change <u>were honoring</u> to <u>will honor</u>
   (5) no correction is necessary

Questions 6 through 9 refer to the following paragraph.

(1) Most people are not familiar with the importance of automobile airbags. (2) A woman in my neighborhood recently seen a terrifying accident in which the driver likely would have been killed if his airbag had not protected him. (3) Instead, he will walk away with only a few bruises and a great deal of gratitude. (4) My neighbor had known that seat belts were important, and she had always buckled up. (5) Until she saw that accident, though, she hasn't thought much about the value of airbags. (6) Now she said she will never again drive or ride in a car without airbags.

6. Sentence 2: **A woman in my neighborhood recently seen a terrifying accident in which the driver likely would have been killed if his airbag had not protected him.**

Which is the best way to write the underlined portion of this sentence? If the original is the best way, choose option (1).

(1) recently seen a terrifying accident
(2) recently had seen a terrifying accident
(3) recently will see a terrifying accident
(4) recently saw a terrifying accident
(5) recently was seeing a terrifying accident

7. Sentence 3: **Instead, he will walk away with only a few bruises and a great deal of gratitude.**

Which correction should be made to sentence 3?

(1) change will walk to walked
(2) change will walk to is walking
(3) change will walk to has walked
(4) change will walk to walk
(5) change will walk to will be walking

8. Sentence 5: **Until she saw that accident, though, she hasn't thought much about the value of airbags.**

Which correction should be made to sentence 5?

(1) change saw to sees
(2) change saw to will see
(3) change hasn't thought to will think
(4) change hasn't thought to isn't thinking
(5) change hasn't thought to hadn't thought

9. Sentence 6: **Now she said she will never again drive or ride in a car without airbags.**

Which correction should be made to sentence 6?

(1) change said to says
(2) change said to will say
(3) change said to had said
(4) change will never again drive to will never again have driven
(5) change will never again drive to will never again be driving

[**TIP**]

Verb tenses signal when events happen. Clue words such as *now*, *last week*, and *next year* also help readers and writers know when an action takes place. Be sure to pay attention to all the clue words in a paragraph so that you can choose correct verb tenses.

Answers and explanations start on page 112.

Skill 7

Sequence of Tenses

The **verb tenses** within a sentence and within a paragraph should be consistent with the action or condition being described. Do not change tenses unless the action or condition requires a change.

When there is more than one verb in a sentence or paragraph, the tense of each verb tells its relationship to the other verbs. Additionally, surrounding sentences and other clue words about time indicate when actions occur, letting you know which tense to use. In deciding on the proper tense, ask yourself these questions: *Do the events or conditions occur at the same time? If the times are different, what is the difference?*

Incorrect: When I <u>see</u> the rising prices of energy, I <u>will wonder</u> how to make ends meet.
Correct: When I <u>see</u> the rising prices of energy, I <u>wonder</u> how to make ends meet.
Explanation: Both verbs, *see* and *wonder*, should be in present tense. Both the seeing and the wondering are taking place in the present.

Incorrect: As we <u>finished</u> each section of the book, we <u>review</u> our notes.
Correct: As we <u>finished</u> each section of the book, we <u>reviewed</u> our notes.
Explanation: In this sentence, both events take place in the past, so both verbs should be in simple past tense.

Incorrect: Although I <u>am</u> not ready yet, I <u>get</u> my dream job eventually.
Correct: Although I <u>am</u> not ready yet, I <u>will get</u> my dream job eventually.
Explanation: Here, the verb *am* tells about a present condition, whereas getting a dream job will happen in the future. These events occur at different times, requiring the use of the present tense and the future tense in the same sentence.

Read the sentence. Choose the <u>one best answer</u> to the question.

Even though I really want that car, I knew buying it is a bad decision.

QUESTION: Which correction should be made to this sentence?

   (1) change <u>knew</u> to <u>will know</u>
   (2) change <u>is</u> to <u>was</u>
   (3) change <u>knew</u> to <u>know</u>
   (4) change <u>want</u> to <u>wanted</u>
   (5) no correction is necessary

EXPLANATIONS

   (1) No. The future-tense verb *will know* is not consistent with the present-tense verbs *want* and *is*.
   (2) No. The past-tense verb *was* may be consistent with the verb *knew*, but it is not consistent with the present-tense verb *want*.
   (3) **Yes. All three verbs, *know*, *want*, and *is*, correctly show a present condition.**
   (4) No. The past-tense verb *wanted* may be consistent with the verb *knew*, but it is not consistent with the present-tense verb *is*.
   (5) No. This option is incorrect because *knew* does not reflect the present.

ANSWER: (3) change <u>knew</u> to <u>know</u>

Practice the Skill

Try these sample questions. Choose the one best answer to each question. Then check your answers and read the explanations.

(1) Heart disease and cancer were major illnesses that affect men and women. (2) They are leading causes of death today. (3) Many scientists are working to cure these conditions. (4) According to the American Heart Society, coronary heart disease is the leading cause of death in the United States. (5) Stroke is the number three cause of death in the United States and a leading cause of serious disability. (6) It's important to reduce risk factors, know the warning signs, and know how to respond quickly and properly if warning signs occur.

1. Sentence 1: **Heart disease and cancer were major illnesses that affect men and women.**

Which correction should be made to sentence 1?

(1) change <u>were</u> to <u>weren't</u>
(2) change <u>were</u> to <u>are</u>
(3) change <u>affect</u> to <u>affects</u>
(4) change <u>were</u> to <u>will be</u>
(5) change <u>affect</u> to <u>affected</u>

HINT Where else in the paragraph can you get information to help you answer this question? Read all material available to help you decide when events or conditions are taking place.

2. Sentence 3: **Many <u>scientists are working</u> to cure these conditions.**

Which is the <u>best</u> way to write the underlined portion of this sentence? If the original is the best way, choose option (1).

(1) scientists are working
(2) scientists were working
(3) scientists worked
(4) scientists will be working
(5) scientists will have worked

HINT What choice is most consistent with information both within the sentence and in surrounding sentences? Choose a verb tense that makes the most sense with both.

Answers and Explanations

1. (2) change <u>were</u> to <u>are</u>
Option (2) correctly uses the present tense to show a present condition. Additionally, the present tense is consistent with the information and verb tenses in the rest of the paragraph.

Option (1) incorrectly changes the meaning of the sentence for no reason. Option (3) does not correct the tense and it creates a problem with subject-verb agreement. Option (4) incorrectly uses the future tense, which is not consistent with the tense of the rest of the paragraph. Option (5) incorrectly uses the simple past tense, which is also not consistent with the rest of the paragraph.

2. (1) scientists are working
Option (1) correctly uses the present continuous verb *are working* to tell about action ongoing in the present. Using a present-tense verb form is consistent with both the verb forms and the tense of the rest of the paragraph, which tells about present conditions and events.

Options (2) and (3) incorrectly use past-tense verbs (the past continuous verb *were working* and the simple past-tense verb *worked*) that are not consistent with the tense of the rest of the paragraph. Options (4) and (5) incorrectly use future-tense verbs that are not consistent with the tense of the rest of the paragraph.

Sequence of Tenses

Directions: Choose the <u>one best answer</u> to each question.

<u>Questions 1 through 5</u> refer to the following paragraph.

(1) An increasing amount of food is exported to the United States and Canada from the countries of South America. (2) For example, Chile grew and exports many varieties of non-tropical fruit, especially apples. (3) Table grapes and lemons are also grown for export. (4) Vineyards planted in the sixteenth century still produce excellent wines. (5) In many kitchens of North America, cooks have came to rely on superb seafood from the waters off Chile's long Pacific coast. (6) The kinds and quantities of food exports will have grown beyond the coffee that we have long enjoyed from South America.

1. Sentence 1: **An increasing amount of food is exported to the United States and Canada from the countries of South America.**

   Which correction should be made to sentence 1?

   (1) change <u>is</u> to <u>was</u>
   (2) change <u>is</u> to <u>had been</u>
   (3) change <u>exported</u> to <u>exports</u>
   (4) change <u>is</u> to <u>were</u>
   (5) no correction is necessary

2. Sentence 2: **For example, Chile grew and exports many varieties of non-tropical fruit, especially apples.**

   Which correction should be made to sentence 2?

   (1) change <u>grew</u> to <u>grown</u>
   (2) change <u>grew</u> to <u>grows</u>
   (3) change <u>exports</u> to <u>exported</u>
   (4) change <u>exports</u> to <u>will export</u>
   (5) no correction is necessary

3. Sentence 4: **Vineyards planted in the sixteenth century <u>still produce</u> excellent wines.**

   Which is the <u>best</u> way to write the underlined portion of this sentence? If the original is the best way, choose option (1).

   (1) still produce
   (2) will still produce
   (3) still produced
   (4) still have produced
   (5) still will be producing

4. Sentence 5: **In many kitchens of North America, cooks have came to rely on superb seafood from the waters off Chile's long Pacific coast.**

   Which correction should be made to sentence 5?

   (1) remove <u>came</u>
   (2) change <u>came to rely</u> to <u>came to relying</u>
   (3) change <u>came</u> to <u>come</u>
   (4) change <u>have came</u> to <u>will come</u>
   (5) no correction is necessary

5. Sentence 6: **The kinds and quantities of food exports <u>will have grown</u> beyond the coffee that we have long enjoyed from South America.**

   Which is the <u>best</u> way to write the underlined portion of this sentence? If the original is the best way, choose option (1).

   (1) will have grown
   (2) have grown
   (3) had grown
   (4) will grow
   (5) grown

Questions 6 through 9 refer to the following paragraph.

(1) The beaches in the southern United States along the Gulf of Mexico are popular destinations for thousands of people each summer. (2) The sun, sand, and surf are great fun. (3) One danger that everyone must look for when the water got very warm and salty is periodic invasions of stinging jellyfish. (4) Activities like wading, fishing, and swimming brought adults and children into contact with these creatures. (5) Jellyfish continue to sting after they are dead, so many stings occurred on land when people step on a jellyfish or try to pick one up. (6) Stings are painful but are usually not dangerous except for people who have allergies.

6. Sentence 3: **One danger that everyone must look for when the water got very warm and salty is periodic invasions of stinging jellyfish.**

Which correction should be made to sentence 3?

(1) change got to gets
(2) insert has before got
(3) change is to had been
(4) change is to are
(5) no correction is necessary

7. Sentence 4: **Activities like wading, fishing, and swimming brought adults and children into contact with these creatures.**

Which is the best way to write the underlined portion of this sentence? If the original is the best way, choose option (1).

(1) brought
(2) had brought
(3) brung
(4) will bring
(5) bring

8. Sentence 5: **Jellyfish continue to sting after they are dead, so many stings occurred on land when people step on a jellyfish or try to pick one up.**

Which is the best way to write the underlined portion of this sentence? If the original is the best way, choose option (1).

(1) occurred
(2) had occurred
(3) could not occur
(4) occur
(5) will have occurred

9. Sentence 6: **Stings are painful but are usually not dangerous except for people who have allergies.**

Which correction should be made to sentence 6?

(1) change are painful to were painful
(2) change are usually to was usually
(3) change have to had
(4) change have to has
(5) no correction is necessary

[**TIP**]

As you read a paragraph, decide when the main action or condition is taking place. Also pay attention to clue words to help you determine if there are shifts in the time frame within a paragraph or sentence. Use verb tenses that are appropriate for each time frame.

Answers and explanations start on page 113.

Subject-Verb Agreement

One writing error that you may see on the GED Writing Test involves **subject-verb agreement.** The subject and a verb in a sentence must agree in number. In other words, the subject and the verb must *both* be **singular** or must *both* be **plural**.

My computer is old. (Both the subject *computer* and the verb *is* are singular.)
My computers are old. (Both the subject *computers* and the verb *are* are plural.)

A **compound subject** whose parts are joined by *and* requires a plural verb.

Subject-Verb Agreement Error: The modem and the disk drive is broken.
Correct Subject-Verb Agreement: The modem and the disk drive <u>are</u> broken.

The plural verb *are* agrees with the compound subject, which is joined by *and*.

When the parts of a compound subject are singular and are joined by *or* or *nor*, the sentence requires a singular verb.

Subject-Verb Agreement Error: Neither the modem nor the disk drive are working.
Correct Subject-Verb Agreement: Neither the modem nor the disk drive <u>is</u> working.

The singular verb *is* agrees with the compound subject, which is joined by *nor*.

When a singular and a plural subject are joined by *or* or *nor*, the verb must agree with the closer subject.

Subject-Verb Agreement Error: Neither the computer nor the printers is working.
Correct Subject-Verb Agreement: Neither the computer nor the printers <u>are</u> working.

The plural verb *are* agrees with the closer subject, *printers*.

Read the sentence below. Choose the <u>one best answer</u> to the question.

The instruction booklet that was sent are missing.

QUESTION: Which correction should be made to this sentence?

   (1) change <u>are</u> to <u>am</u>
   (2) change <u>was</u> to <u>were</u>
   (3) change <u>are</u> to <u>is</u>
   (4) change <u>that</u> to <u>what</u>
   (5) no correction is necessary

EXPLANATIONS

   (1) No. *Am* is a singular verb but should be used only when the subject is *I*.
   (2) No. The singular noun *booklet* requires a singular verb, not the plural verb *were*.
   (3) **Yes. The singular subject *booklet* requires a singular verb, *is*.**
   (4) No. *That* is a pronoun that correctly stands for the singular noun *booklet*.
   (5) No. The singular subject *booklet* requires a singular verb.

ANSWER: (3) change <u>are</u> to <u>is</u>

Practice the Skill

Try these sample questions. Choose the <u>one best answer</u> to each question. Then check your answers and read the explanations.

(1) Neither seeds nor water is optional if you are a gardener. (2) Unfortunately, some hard work is also necessary. (3) In the end, beautiful flowers and delicious food rewards you for all your work.

1. Sentence 1: **Neither seeds nor water is optional if you are a gardener.**

   Which correction should be made to sentence 1?

   (1) change <u>is</u> to <u>are</u>
   (2) change <u>is</u> to <u>am</u>
   (3) change <u>is</u> to <u>were</u>
   (4) change <u>is</u> to <u>be</u>
   (5) no correction is necessary

   HINT What is the subject of the sentence? Remember, when singular and plural subjects are joined by *or* or *nor*, the verb agrees with the closest subject.

2. Sentence 3: **In the end, beautiful flowers and delicious food rewards you for all your work.**

   Which correction should be made to sentence 3?

   (1) change <u>rewards</u> to <u>rewarded</u>
   (2) change <u>rewards</u> to <u>rewarding</u>
   (3) change <u>rewards</u> to <u>have rewarded</u>
   (4) change <u>rewards</u> to <u>reward</u>
   (5) no correction is necessary

   HINT What verb form should you have for a compound subject joined with *and*?

Answers and Explanations

1. (5) no correction is necessary
Option (5) correctly uses the singular verb *is*. The compound subject is joined by *nor* and the subject closest to the verb is the singular *water*.

Option (1) incorrectly uses the plural verb *are*, which does not agree in number with the closest subject, *water*. Option (2) incorrectly uses a verb that should be used only with the word *I*. Option (3) incorrectly suggests *were*, which should be used only with plural subjects or the subject *you*. Option (4) incorrectly suggests the verb *be*, which does not make sense in the sentence.

2. (4) change <u>rewards</u> to <u>reward</u>
Option (4) correctly changes the singular verb *rewards* to the plural *reward* to agree with the compound subject that is joined by *and*.

Options (1) and (2) incorrectly suggest the past tense *rewarded* and present continuous tense *rewarding*, but neither of those forms makes sense in context with the rest of the passage. Option (3) is incorrect because the present perfect verb *have rewarded* is not consistent with the tense of the whole passage. Option (5) is not correct because the compound subject is joined by *and* and requires a plural verb, not the singular verb *rewards*.

Subject-Verb Agreement

Directions: Choose the one best answer to each question.

Questions 1 through 4 refer to the following paragraph.

    (1) Neither drinking nor sleeping mixes with driving. (2) Some experts view being sleepy behind the wheel as similar to being intoxicated. (3) Driving at night or driving when you're tired increase the likelihood of an accident. (4) There is some common danger signs that you are about to fall asleep while driving. (5) Yawning, nodding, and seeing double are three signs of fatigue. (6) Driving off the road and jerking the car back into the lane also means you are in danger.

1. Sentence 2: **Some experts view being sleepy behind the wheel as similar to being intoxicated.**

   If you rewrote sentence 2 beginning with <u>According to some experts, being sleepy behind the wheel</u> the next word should be

   (1) views
   (2) is
   (3) are
   (4) was
   (5) being

2. Sentence 3: **Driving at night or driving when you're tired increase the likelihood of an accident.**

   Which correction should be made to sentence 3?

   (1) change <u>you're</u> to <u>you was</u>
   (2) change <u>driving when</u> to <u>having driven when</u>
   (3) change <u>you're</u> to <u>you is</u>
   (4) change <u>increase</u> to <u>increases</u>
   (5) no correction is necessary

3. Sentence 4: **There <u>is</u> some common danger signs that you are about to fall asleep while driving.**

   Which is the <u>best</u> way to write the underlined portion of this sentence? If the original is the best way, choose option (1).

   (1) is
   (2) are
   (3) were
   (4) has been
   (5) have been

4. Sentence 6: **Driving off the road and jerking the car back into the lane also means you are in danger.**

   Which correction should be made to sentence 6?

   (1) change <u>you are</u> to <u>you is</u>
   (2) change <u>you are</u> to <u>you am</u>
   (3) change <u>means</u> to <u>mean</u>
   (4) change <u>means</u> to <u>meant</u>
   (5) no correction is necessary

> **TIP**
>
> Subject-verb agreement errors are common in sentences that begin with *There is* or *There are*. Writers and readers must look ahead to the subject, which comes after the verb in this type of sentence. For example, in the sentence *There are many reasons for being late*, the plural subject *reasons* requires the plural verb *are*.

Questions 5 through 9 refer to the following paragraph.

(1) Flour, sugar, and shortening is essential ingredients for the home baker. (2) They serves as the basis for most types of cakes and cookies. (3) In addition, either baking powder or baking soda are needed. (4) These substances are leavening agents, and they make cakes and cookies rise as they bake. (5) Neither butter nor milk are necessary for most baking projects. (6) Some bakers, though, consider these dairy products essential to the best recipes.

5. Sentence 1: **Flour, sugar, and shortening is essential ingredients for the home baker.**

   Which correction should be made to sentence 1?

   (1) change is to were
   (2) change is to was
   (3) change is to have been
   (4) change is to am
   (5) change is to are

6. Sentence 2: **They serves as the basis for most types of cakes and cookies.**

   Which is the best way to write the underlined portion of this sentence? If the original is the best way, choose option (1).

   (1) serves
   (2) will serves
   (3) served
   (4) serve
   (5) have served

7. Sentence 3: **In addition, either baking powder or baking soda are needed.**

   Which correction should be made to sentence 3?

   (1) change are to is
   (2) change are to am
   (3) change are to were
   (4) change are to shall be
   (5) no correction is necessary

8. Sentence 4: **These substances are leavening agents, and they make cakes and cookies rise as they bake.**

   Which is the best way to write the underlined portion of this sentence? If the original is the best way, choose option (1).

   (1) are leavening agents, and they make
   (2) is leavening agents, and they make
   (3) is leavening agents, and they makes
   (4) are leavening agents, and they makes
   (5) are leavening agents, and they made

9. Sentence 5: **Neither butter nor milk are necessary for most baking projects.**

   Which correction should be made to sentence 5?

   (1) change are to has been
   (2) change are to is
   (3) change are to have been
   (4) change are to am
   (5) change are to were

Answers and explanations start on page 113.

Skill 9

Common Agreement Problems

Some questions on the GED Writing Test will ask you to determine whether subjects and verbs in sentences agree. In certain types of sentences, **subject-verb agreement** errors are common.

In a sentence with an **interrupting phrase**, a group of words separates the **subject** and the **verb**.

Example: <u>Biscuits</u>, a common breakfast treat, <u>are</u> simple to make.
Explanation: The subject of this sentence is *Biscuits*, which is separated from the verb by the interrupting phrase *a common breakfast treat*. The plural verb *are* is required for agreement.

In a sentence with an **inverted sentence structure**, the subject comes after the verb. Questions often have inverted sentence structure.

Example: <u>Are</u> your <u>answers</u> all correct?
Explanation: The subject of this sentence is *answers*. The plural verb *Are* is required for agreement.

Example: Near the top of the page <u>is</u> the <u>date</u> of the letter.
Explanation: The subject of this sentence is *date*; the singular verb *is* is required for agreement. If the sentence is not inverted, it becomes easy to see the subject and verb: *The <u>date</u> of the letter <u>is</u> near the top of the page.*

In a **sentence that begins with *Here* or *There*,** the subject comes after the verb. The word *here* or *there* is never the subject of a sentence.

Example: Here <u>is</u> the best <u>book</u> in the library.
Explanation: The subject of this sentence is *book*; *is* is the singular verb.

Example: There <u>are</u> many <u>reasons</u> to go to the library.
Explanation: The subject of the sentence is *reasons*; *are* is the singular verb.

Read the sentence below. Choose the <u>one best answer</u> to the question.

The apartments I want you to see is just around the corner.

QUESTION: Which correction should be made to this sentence?

    (1) change <u>is</u> to <u>are</u>
    (2) change <u>is</u> to <u>am</u>
    (3) change <u>want</u> to <u>wants</u>
    (4) change <u>want</u> to <u>wanted</u>
    (5) change <u>see</u> to <u>sees</u>

EXPLANATIONS

    (1) **Yes. The plural subject *apartments* requires a plural verb, *are*.**
    (2) No. The plural subject *apartments* requires a plural verb, not the singular verb *am*, which should be used only when the subject is *I*.
    (3) No. The singular verb *want* agrees with *I*, which is the subject of the group of words that interrupts the main subject and verb of the sentence.
    (4) No. The past-tense verb *wanted* is not consistent with the rest of the sentence.
    (5) No. *See* is correct in the original sentence and should not be changed.

ANSWER: (1) change <u>is</u> to <u>are</u>

Practice the Skill

Try these sample questions. Choose the one best answer to each question. Then check your answers and read the explanations.

(1) Among the experiences possible in Swedish Lapland are the chance to stay in a hotel built entirely of ice. (2) There has been many people curious to visit this unusual hotel. (3) They do not know what to expect upon arrival, but the ice hotel peeks their interest. (4) The number of visitors has increased every year since its opening.

1. Sentence 1: **Among the experiences possible in Swedish Lapland are the chance to stay in a hotel built entirely of ice.**

   Which correction should be made to sentence 1?

   (1) change experiences to experience
   (2) change are to is
   (3) change stay to stays
   (4) change built to build
   (5) no correction is necessary

   HINT Find the subject of the sentence. In this inverted sentence, the subject is *chance*. Then find the verb and see if it agrees with the subject.

2. Sentence 2: **There has been many people curious to visit this unusual hotel.**

   Which correction should be made to sentence 2?

   (1) change has to was
   (2) change has to is
   (3) change has to have
   (4) change has to were
   (5) change has to are

   HINT Remember that when a sentence begins with *There*, the subject will come later in the sentence, after the verb. Find the subject first. Then locate the verb and see if it agrees with the subject.

Answers and Explanations

1. (2) change are to is
Option (2) is correct because the singular subject *chance* requires a singular verb, *is*.

Option (1) incorrectly changes the plural *experiences* to the singular *experience*, although the word *Among* indicates that a plural noun is required. Option (3) is incorrect because it changes the verb to *stays*, which does not agree with the tense of the rest of the sentence. Option (4) incorrectly introduces the present-tense verb *build*, whereas the subject of the clause is a hotel that is already built. Option (5) is not correct because the singular subject requires a singular verb, not the plural verb *are*.

2. (3) change has to have
Option (3) is correct because the plural subject *people* requires a plural verb, *have been*.

Options (1) and (2) are incorrect because neither *was been* nor *is been* makes sense as a verb. Options (4) and (5) suggest plural verbs, *were* and *are*, but *were been* and *are been* do not make sense as verbs.

Common Agreement Problems

Directions: Choose the one best answer to each question.

Questions 1 through 5 refer to the following paragraph.

(1) Along with the many advantages of credit cards exists potential pitfalls. (2) Despite the convenience of using credit cards, the total cost of the many things we charge add up fast. (3) There's too many of us who have enormous credit card debts. (4) The best thing we can do for ourselves is pay off the balances as quickly as possible. (5) How much does our financial situations suffer from large credit card balances? (6) The money we pay in interest charges could be going into our pockets instead.

1. Sentence 1: **Along with the many advantages of credit cards exists potential pitfalls.**

   Which correction should be made to sentence 1?

   (1) change advantages to advantage
   (2) change cards to card
   (3) change exists to exist
   (4) change exists to existing
   (5) change exists to existed

2. Sentence 2: **Despite the convenience of using credit cards, the total cost of the many things we charge add up fast.**

   Which is the best way to write the underlined portion of this sentence? If the original is the best way, choose option (1).

   (1) things we charge add
   (2) things we charges add
   (3) thing we charge add
   (4) things we charge added
   (5) things we charge adds

3. Sentence 3: **There's too many of us who have enormous credit card debts.**

   Which correction should be made to sentence 3?

   (1) change There's to There is
   (2) change There's to There are
   (3) change There's to There were
   (4) change have to is
   (5) change have to had

4. Sentence 4: **The best thing we can do for ourselves is pay off the balances as quickly as possible.**

   If you rewrote sentence 4 beginning with Paying off the balances as quickly as possible the next word(s) should be

   (1) is
   (2) was
   (3) will be
   (4) are
   (5) has been

5. Sentence 5: **How much does our financial situations suffer from large credit card balances?**

   Which is the best way to write the underlined portion of this sentence? If the original is the best way, choose option (1).

   (1) does our financial situations suffer
   (2) do our financial situations suffer
   (3) did our financial situations suffer
   (4) will our financial situations suffer
   (5) does our financial situations suffers

Questions 6 through 9 refer to the following paragraph.

(1) Opposite the Vietnam Veterans Memorial and near the Lincoln Memorial in Washington, D.C., are the newer Korean War Veterans Memorial. (2) It honors the 1.7 million Americans who served and the more than 54,000 who died in the Korean War from 1950 to 1953. (3) This conflict came soon after World War II and before the Vietnam War. (4) Overshadowed by both these events, it has been called the forgotten war. (5) However, the Korean War Veterans Memorial, dedicated 42 years after the war's end, now reminds visitors of that war. (6) Reflected in a long, black granite wall is nineteen soldiers trudging uphill. (7) There is an inscription engraved at the end of the wall that reads, "Freedom Is Not Free."

6. Sentence 1: **Opposite the Vietnam Veterans Memorial and near the Lincoln Memorial in Washington, D.C., are the newer Korean War Veterans Memorial.**

Which correction should be made to sentence 1?

(1) change <u>are</u> to <u>is</u>
(2) change <u>are</u> to <u>be</u>
(3) change <u>are</u> to <u>were</u>
(4) change <u>are</u> to <u>was</u>
(5) change <u>are</u> to <u>had been</u>

7. Sentence 5: **However, the Korean War Veterans Memorial, <u>dedicated 42 years after the war's end, now reminds</u> visitors of that war.**

Which is the <u>best</u> way to write the underlined portion of this sentence? If the original is the best way, choose option (1).

(1) dedicated 42 years after the war's end, now reminds
(2) dedicates 42 years after the war's end, now reminds
(3) dedicated 42 years after the war's end, now remind
(4) dedicated 42 years after the war's ends, now reminds
(5) dedicating 42 years after the war's end, now reminds

8. Sentence 6: **Reflected in a long, black granite wall is nineteen soldiers trudging uphill.**

Which correction should be made to sentence 6?

(1) change <u>wall</u> to <u>walls</u>
(2) change <u>is</u> to <u>are</u>
(3) change <u>is</u> to <u>was</u>
(4) change <u>trudging</u> to <u>trudged</u>
(5) no correction is necessary

9. Sentence 7: **There is an inscription engraved at the end of the wall that reads, "Freedom Is Not Free."**

Which correction should be made to sentence 7?

(1) change <u>is</u> to <u>are</u>
(2) change <u>is</u> to <u>were</u>
(3) change <u>engraved</u> to <u>engraves</u>
(4) change <u>reads</u> to <u>read</u>
(5) no correction is necessary

> **TIP**
>
> In order to determine subject-verb agreement of a sentence that has an interrupting phrase between the subject and the verb, read the sentence without the interrupting phrase. Hearing the subject and the verb close together will help you identify whether there is subject-verb agreement.

Answers and explanations start on page 114.

Usage

Pronouns

A **pronoun** is a word that takes the place of a **noun** in a sentence. A **personal pronoun** refers to a person or persons. The form of a pronoun depends on the way the pronoun is used.

> **Subject Pronouns:** I, you, he, she, it, we, they
> **Object Pronouns:** me, you, him, her, it, us, them
> **Possessive Pronouns (before nouns):** my, your, his, her, its, our, their
> **Possessive Pronouns (after verbs):** mine, yours, his, hers, its, ours, theirs

The form of the pronoun must be correct for its function in the sentence.

> **Incorrect:** Julie and me finally got our chance to see a game in Fenway Park.
> **Correct:** Julie and I finally got our chance to see a game in Fenway Park.
> **Explanation:** Because the pronoun functions as part of the subject of the sentence, the subject pronoun *I* is necessary.

Another way to think about pronouns is according to person. **Person** refers to the form a pronoun takes depending on whether the pronoun refers to the speaker (first person), the one(s) spoken to (second person), or the one(s) spoken about (third person).

> **First-Person Pronouns:** I, me, my, mine, we, us, our, ours
> **Second-Person Pronouns:** you, your, yours
> **Third-Person Pronouns:** he, him, his, she, her, hers, it, its, they, them, theirs

A common pronoun error is a shift in the person or pronouns in a sentence.

> **Incorrect:** We like that electronics store's staff because they won't pressure you.
> **Correct:** We like that electronics store's staff because they won't pressure us.
> **Explanation:** The incorrect sentence shifts from first-person *we* to second-person *you*. Shifts like this one can confuse meaning. Changing *you* to first-person *us* makes the sentence clear.

Read the sentence below. Choose the one best answer to the question.

Him is the one you need to talk to in order to get information about your job.

QUESTION: Which correction should be made to this sentence?

    (1) change you to yours
    (2) change Him to He
    (3) change one to manager
    (4) change your to our
    (5) no correction is necessary

EXPLANATIONS

    (1) No. *Yours* is a possessive pronoun, which would not make sense in this case.
    (2) **Yes. *He* is a subject pronoun, correctly used as the subject.**
    (3) No. This option unnecessarily changes the meaning of the sentence.
    (4) No. This option unnecessarily changes the meaning of the sentence.
    (5) No. The original incorrectly uses the object pronoun *Him* as its subject.

ANSWER: (2) change Him to He

Practice the Skill

Try these sample questions. Choose the one best answer to each question. Then check your answers and read the explanations.

(1) Regardless of the weather, both my wife and me try to exercise regularly. (2) When you don't get adequate exercise, our health will eventually suffer.

1. Sentence 1: **Regardless of the weather, both my wife and me try to exercise regularly.**

   Which correction should be made to sentence 1?

   (1) change <u>my wife and me</u> to <u>me and my wife</u>
   (2) change <u>wife</u> to <u>she</u>
   (3) remove <u>both</u>
   (4) change <u>me</u> to <u>I</u>
   (5) no correction is necessary

   HINT What is the subject of the sentence? What kind of pronoun should be used for a subject?

2. Sentence 2: **When you don't get adequate exercise, <u>our</u> health will eventually suffer.**

   What is the <u>best</u> way to write the underlined portion of this sentence? If the original is the best way, choose option (1).

   (1) our
   (2) their
   (3) your
   (4) my
   (5) her

   HINT Are there other pronouns used in the sentence? What pronoun could you use to make the sentence consistent? Be sure to choose a pronoun that makes sense.

Answers and Explanations

1. (4) change <u>me</u> to <u>I</u>
Option (4) is correct because the pronoun functions as part of the subject of the sentence, and therefore the subject pronoun *I* is necessary.

Option (1) is incorrect because a subject pronoun is required. Option (2) substitutes a pronoun for *my wife*, which unnecessarily makes it unclear who is exercising with the speaker. Option (3) is incorrect because removing *both* does not correct the erroneous pronoun *me*. Option (5) incorrectly uses *me*, an object pronoun, as a subject.

2. (3) your
Option (3) uses the second-person pronoun *your*, which is consistent with the pronoun *you* used earlier in the sentence.

Options (1), (2), (4), and (5) are incorrect because none of the choices (*our, their, my, her*) is consistent with the previous second-person pronoun *you*.

Pronouns

Directions: Choose the one best answer to each question.

Questions 1 through 5 refer to the following paragraph.

(1) Experts are now advising all of us who are computer users to place their monitors below eye level and tilted away from the face. (2) We can then read our monitors as they would read a magazine. (3) Your monitors are often placed too high. (4) People assume that you read best at eye level, but you don't. (5) If my monitor is too high, I feel pain in my neck and shoulders. (6) If you have had similar experiences, then you and me should pay attention to this new information. (7) I plan to change my habits; join me by changing yours.

1. Sentence 1: **Experts are now advising all of us who are computer users to place their monitors below eye level and tilted away from the face.**

   What is the best way to write the underlined portion of this sentence? If the original is the best way, choose option (1).

   (1) their
   (2) them
   (3) they
   (4) our
   (5) my

2. Sentence 2: **We can then read our monitors as they would read a magazine.**

   Which correction should be made to sentence 2?

   (1) replace We with You
   (2) replace our with your
   (3) replace they with we
   (4) replace a magazine with magazines
   (5) no correction is necessary

3. Sentence 3: **Your monitors are often placed too high.**

   Which correction should be made to sentence 3?

   (1) replace Your with Our
   (2) insert they after monitors
   (3) replace Your with My
   (4) replace Your with Their
   (5) no correction is necessary

4. Sentence 4: **People assume that you read best at eye level, but you don't.**

   Which correction should be made to sentence 4?

   (1) replace the first you with I
   (2) replace the first you with we
   (3) replace the second you with they
   (4) replace the second you with we
   (5) no correction is necessary

5. Sentence 6: **If you have had similar experiences, then you and me should pay attention to this new information.**

   What is the best way to write the underlined portion of this sentence? If the original is the best way, choose option (1).

   (1) you and me
   (2) you and I
   (3) they
   (4) yours
   (5) I

Questions 6 through 9 refer to the following paragraph.

(1) The polite behavior, or manners, expected of young people has changed greatly over the years. (2) During the fifteenth century, children were expected to stand continuously in the presence of they parents and to kneel in the presence of teachers. (3) In the seventeenth and eighteenth centuries, the rules about meeting people were different. (4) A young man could not speak to a young woman until he had been properly introduced. (5) Until then, she and him could only glance at each other hopefully. (6) Today, rules are much less rigid, but it does exist in some form. (7) We must know and follow customs if you want to be accepted by others.

6. Sentence 2: **During the fifteenth century, children were expected to stand continuously in the presence of they parents and to kneel in the presence of teachers.**

Which correction should be made to sentence 2?

(1) change they to them
(2) change they to their
(3) change they to our
(4) change they to us
(5) no correction is necessary

7. Sentence 5: **Until then, she and him could only glance at each other hopefully.**

Which correction should be made to sentence 5?

(1) change she to her
(2) change him to he
(3) change she and him to we
(4) change she and him to him and she
(5) no correction is necessary

8. Sentence 6: **Today, rules are much less rigid, but it does exist in some form.**

What is the best way to write the underlined portion of this sentence? If the original is the best way, choose option (1).

(1) it does
(2) their does
(3) there does
(4) its does
(5) they do

9. Sentence 7: **We must know and follow customs if you want to be accepted by others.**

What is the best way to write the underlined portion of this sentence? If the original is the best way, choose option 1.

(1) you
(2) they
(3) we
(4) your
(5) their

TIP

Use the meaning of the sentence, the meaning of other nearby sentences, and other pronouns to help you decide whether a first-, second-, or third-person pronoun is appropriate for the meaning of a sentence. Then choose the form that is most consistent with the meaning of the sentence and surrounding sentences.

Answers and explanations start on page 115.

Usage

Pronouns and Antecedents

On the GED Writing Test, you may see questions about pronouns and antecedents. A **pronoun** is a word that takes the place of a **noun**. The **antecedent** is the word that the pronoun refers to. For the meaning of a pronoun to be clear, its antecedent must be clear.

Avoid vague missing pronoun references. Be sure the antecedent is fully expressed.

> **Incorrect:** The deep water in the middle made <u>it</u> colder than he had expected.
> **Correct:** The deep water in the middle of the <u>pond</u> made <u>it</u> colder than he had expected.
> **Explanation:** In the incorrect example, *it* has no clear antecedent.

To make meaning clear, be sure a pronoun refers to only one possible antecedent.

> **Incorrect:** Her mother wanted to go with Eileen, but <u>she</u> couldn't go.
> **Explanation:** In this example, it is unclear whether *she* is Eileen or her mother.
> **Correct:** Eileen's mother wanted to go with <u>her</u>, but <u>Eileen</u> couldn't go.
> **Correct:** Although Eileen's <u>mother</u> wanted to go, <u>she</u> was unable to do so.
> **Explanation:** In the correct examples, the antecedents are clear. In the first example, it is Eileen who couldn't go; in the second, it is Eileen's mother who couldn't go.

Pronouns must agree in number with their antecedents.

> **Incorrect:** Each <u>student</u> should prepare well so <u>they</u> can do well on the test.
> **Explanation:** *Student* is singular; *they* is a plural pronoun. They do not agree.
> **Correct:** All <u>students</u> should prepare well so <u>they</u> can do well on the test.
> **Correct:** Each <u>student</u> should prepare well so <u>he</u> or <u>she</u> can do well on the test.
> **Explanation:** Either make the antecedent plural to match the plural pronoun, or make the pronoun(s) singular to match the singular antecedent.

Read the sentence below. Choose the <u>one best answer</u> to the question.

Energy prices are high, but it is mostly beyond your control.

QUESTION: Which correction should be made to this sentence?

(1) change <u>are</u> to <u>is</u>
(2) change <u>your</u> to <u>our</u>
(3) change <u>your</u> to <u>their</u>
(4) change <u>it is</u> to <u>they are</u>
(5) no correction is necessary

EXPLANATIONS

(1) No. Neither the singular verb *is* nor the singular pronoun *it* agree with the plural subject *prices*.
(2) No. This change does not fix the error of pronoun/antecedent agreement.
(3) No. This change does not fix the error of pronoun/antecedent agreement.
(4) **Yes. The plural pronoun *they* agrees with the plural antecedent *prices*, and the plural verb *are* agrees with the pronoun *they*.**
(5) No. This is incorrect because *it* is singular, and the antecedent *prices* is plural.

ANSWER: (4) change <u>it is</u> to <u>they are</u>

Practice the Skill

Try these sample questions. Choose the <u>one best answer</u> to each question. Then check your answers and read the explanations.

(1) Both assembly workers and managers think they know how to run the company best. (2) The company president is careful to give them a voice in how the company is run. (3) Each employee has the opportunity to state their opinion.

1. Sentence 2: The company president is careful to give them a voice in how the company is run.

Which correction should be made to sentence 2?

(1) replace <u>them</u> with <u>us</u>
(2) replace <u>The company president</u> with <u>He</u>
(3) replace <u>them</u> with <u>employees</u>
(4) replace <u>the company is</u> with <u>things are</u>
(5) no correction is necessary

HINT Find an antecedent for every pronoun within a sentence. If you cannot, or if the antecedent is unclear, the sentence needs to be corrected.

2. Sentence 3: Each employee has the opportunity to state their opinion.

Which correction should be made to sentence 3?

(1) replace <u>their</u> with <u>our</u>
(2) replace <u>their</u> with <u>they</u>
(3) replace <u>employee</u> with <u>employees</u>
(4) replace <u>their</u> with <u>his or her</u>
(5) no correction is necessary

HINT Decide whether a pronoun is singular or plural. Then determine whether its antecedent is singular or plural. If the two do not agree, then either the antecedent or the pronoun must be changed.

Answers and Explanations

1. (3) replace <u>them</u> with <u>employees</u>
Option (3) replaces the pronoun with a noun because there is no clear antecedent for *them*.

Option (1) is incorrect because the first-person pronoun *us* is not consistent with other nouns and pronouns used in the paragraph. Option (2) incorrectly suggests replacing a noun with a pronoun, *He,* for which there would be no clear antecedent; this change would also not clarify the antecedent of the pronoun *them*. Option (4) incorrectly replaces the noun *company* with *things*, which is vague; this change would also not clarify the antecedent of the pronoun *them*. Option (5) is incorrect because the pronoun *them* has no clear antecedent.

2. (4) replace <u>their</u> with <u>his or her</u>
Option (4) correctly uses singular pronouns *his or her*, which agree with the singular noun *employee*.

Option (1) is incorrect because the plural pronoun *our* neither agrees in number with the antecedent *employee* nor is consistent with other nouns and pronouns used in the paragraph. Option (2) is incorrect because *they* is a plural subject pronoun used where a singular possessive pronoun is needed. Options (3) is incorrect because the plural *employees* does not make sense with the singular adjective *each*, which indicates the antecedent needs to be a singular noun. Option (5) is incorrect because the plural pronoun *their* does not agree with the singular antecedent *employee*.

Skill 11: Pronouns and Antecedents **51**

Pronouns and Antecedents

Directions: Choose the one best answer to each question.

Questions 1 through 5 refer to the following paragraph.

(1) Writing routine business letters is not always easy, and many people avoid the task. (2) If you can learn some basic principles, however, they say you can write effective letters. (3) Anyone can improve their business letters. (4) A writer can tell readers what they want to say by using some simple guidelines. (5) Put the main idea of it in a short first paragraph. (6) Put each detail in a short middle paragraph and close the letter with a short paragraph that restates the main idea. (7) If you write clearly and definitively, everyone will know what you want to communicate.

1. Sentence 2: **If you can learn some basic principles, however, they say you can write effective letters.**

   Which is the best way to write the underlined portion of this sentence? If the original is the best way, choose option (1).

   (1) they say you can
   (2) I can
   (3) we can
   (4) they can
   (5) you can

2. Sentence 3: **Anyone can improve their business letters.**

   Which correction should be made to sentence 3?

   (1) replace Anyone with You
   (2) replace their with they
   (3) remove their
   (4) replace their with our
   (5) no correction is necessary

3. Sentence 4: **A writer can tell readers what they want to say by using some simple guidelines.**

   Which correction should be made to sentence 4?

   (1) replace they want with he or she wants
   (2) replace they with you
   (3) replace some with these
   (4) replace readers with us
   (5) no correction is necessary

4. Sentence 5: **Put the main idea of it in a short first paragraph.**

   Which correction should be made to sentence 5?

   (1) replace it with that
   (2) replace the main idea with its main idea
   (3) replace it with the letter
   (4) replace the with your
   (5) no correction is necessary

5. Sentence 7: **If you write clearly and definitively, everyone will know what you want to communicate.**

   Which correction should be made to sentence 7?

   (1) replace everyone with someone
   (2) replace you with we
   (3) replace what with how
   (4) replace everyone with he and she
   (5) no correction is necessary

Questions 6 through 9 refer to the following paragraph.

(1) Bridge is a popular card game. (2) Each of the four players in a bridge game is paired with their partner. (3) The partners sit across from each other, and when it is dealt, they bid for the right to decide which suit will be the trump suit. (4) Any of the four suits—hearts, spades, diamonds, or clubs—can be the trump suit; a game may also be played without a trump suit. (5) They also bid to win a certain number of tricks. (6) Then each player plays one card at a time, and the highest card wins the trick. (7) The winning partners either take all the cards they said they would, or stop their opponents from doing so.

6. Sentence 2: **Each of the four players in a bridge game is paired with their partner.**

   Which correction should be made to sentence 2?

   (1) change their to his
   (2) change their to a
   (3) change Each to All
   (4) change is to are
   (5) no correction is necessary

7. Sentence 3: **The partners sit across from each other, and when it is dealt, they bid for the right to decide which suit will be the trump suit.**

   Which is the best way to write the underlined portion of this sentence? If the original is the best way, choose option (1).

   (1) each other, and when it is dealt
   (2) them, and when it is dealt
   (3) each other, and when they are dealt
   (4) each other, and when cards are dealt
   (5) each other, and when you deal

8. Sentence 5: **They also bid to win a certain number of tricks.**

   Which correction should be made to sentence 5?

   (1) change They to The players
   (2) change a to their
   (3) insert their before tricks
   (4) change They to You
   (5) remove a certain number of

9. Sentence 7: **The winning partners either take all the cards they said they would, or stop their opponents from doing so.**

   Which is the best way to write the underlined portion of this sentence? If the original is the best way, choose option (1).

   (1) they said they would, or stop their opponents
   (2) they said he or she would, or stop their opponents
   (3) they said they would, or stop our opponents
   (4) they said they would, or stop them opponents
   (5) he said he would, or stop his opponents

TIP

Words such as *everyone, everybody, no one, nobody, anyone, anybody,* and *somebody* are singular, and should be referred to by a singular pronoun.

Answers and explanations start on page 115.

Skill 12

Apostrophes

On the GED Writing Test, you may see questions about the use of apostrophes. An **apostrophe** is a punctuation mark used to show the absence of a letter or letters in a **contraction.** Apostrophes are also used to form the **possessive** of nouns/pronouns.

Apostrophes in Contractions

A contraction combines two words but leaves out one or more letters. An **apostrophe** (') takes the place of the missing letter(s).

Some contractions combine a pronoun and a common verb.

Examples: she + will = she'll   you + are = you're   they + have = they've

Other contractions combine a verb and the word *not*:

Examples: is + not = isn't   do + not = don't   have + not = haven't

Apostrophes in Possessives

Possessive words show ownership. The position of the apostrophe in a possessive noun depends on the kind of noun used to form the possessive.

Possessive singular noun: Add an apostrophe and *s* to a singular noun.
Example: Each <u>citizen's</u> vote should count.

Possessive plural noun: Add only an apostrophe to a plural noun that ends in *s*.
Example: Children may also shape their <u>parents'</u> opinions.

Possessive irregular plural noun: Add an apostrophe and *s* to an irregular plural noun that does not end in *s*.
Example: Parents often shape their <u>children's</u> opinions.

Possessive pronouns show possession, but do not use apostrophes.
Examples: its, your, yours, his, hers, ours, their, theirs, whose

Read the sentence below. Choose the <u>one best answer</u> to the question.

All of my neighbor's lawns look greener than mine.

QUESTION: Which correction should be made to this sentence?

   (1) change <u>neighbor's</u> to <u>neighbor'</u>
   (2) change <u>neighbor's</u> to <u>neighbors</u>
   (3) change <u>neighbor's</u> to <u>neighbors'</u>
   (4) change <u>lawns</u> to <u>lawn's</u>
   (5) change <u>lawns</u> to <u>lawns'</u>

EXPLANATIONS

   (1) No. Adding an apostrophe but no *s* to a singular noun does not correctly form a possessive noun.
   (2) No. *Neighbors* is a plural noun but a possessive noun is needed.
   (3) **Yes. The lawns belong to all of the neighbors, so the correct form is the plural possessive, *neighbors'*.**
   (4) No. The word *lawns* should not be changed to the singular possessive.
   (5) No. It does not make sense for *lawns* to be changed to the plural possessive.

ANSWER: (3) change <u>neighbor's</u> to <u>neighbors'</u>

Practice the Skill

Try these sample questions. Choose the <u>one best answer</u> to each question. Then check your answers and read the explanations.

(1) In the United States, a persons right to vote is not always highly regarded. (2) Most Americans do not express opinions about candidates and election issues. (3) Presidential debates do not attract a large number of viewers and have low ratings. (4) On election days, however, voter turn-out is'nt very high. (5) On average, only 4 out of every 10 registered voters actually votes.

1. Sentence 1: **In the United States, a persons right to vote is not always highly regarded.**

   Which correction should be made to sentence 1?

   (1) change <u>States</u> to <u>States'</u>
   (2) change <u>States</u> to <u>State's</u>
   (3) change <u>persons</u> to <u>persons'</u>
   (4) change <u>persons</u> to <u>person's</u>
   (5) no change is necessary

   HINT To create a singular possessive noun, add an apostrophe and *s* to the noun to show possession.

2. Sentence 4: **On election days, however, voter turn-out is'nt very high.**

   Which correction should be made to sentence 4?

   (1) change <u>days</u> to <u>days'</u>
   (2) change <u>days</u> to <u>day's</u>
   (3) change <u>is'nt</u> to <u>isnt</u>
   (4) change <u>is'nt</u> to <u>isnt'</u>
   (5) change <u>is'nt</u> to <u>isn't</u>

   HINT Remember that the apostrophe in a contraction replaces the letters that are missing. Consider the two words that make up the contraction. Then form the contraction again from those two words, placing the apostrophe where the missing letters would be.

Answers and Explanations

1. (4) change <u>persons</u> to <u>person's</u>
Option (4) correctly forms the singular possessive noun by adding an apostrophe and *s* to the noun *person*.

Options (1) and (2) are incorrect because it does not make sense in the sentence for *States* to be possessive. Option (3) is incorrect because the word *a* indicates that a singular noun is needed, and *persons'* is not a correctly formed singular possessive noun. Option (5) is not correct because an apostrophe is missing from the word *persons*.

2. (5) change <u>is'nt</u> to <u>isn't</u>
Option (5) correctly fixes the misplaced apostrophe in the contraction *isn't* (a combination of *is* and *not*, with the apostrophe taking the place of the *o*).

Options (1) and (2) incorrectly make *days* into a plural possessive and a singular possessive noun, neither of which makes sense in the context of the sentence. Option (3) is incorrect because it omits the apostrophe needed in *isn't*. Option (4) incorrectly places the apostrophe at the end of the contraction instead of where the missing *o* would be.

Apostrophes

Directions: Choose the <u>one best answer</u> to each question.

<u>Questions 1 through 5</u> refer to the following paragraph.

(1) If you've had problems paying bills, you may be the recipient of a collection agencys' attention. (2) In the past, such agencies were'nt regulated by law, and they often harassed people. (3) For that reason, the government has told these agencies what theyre allowed to do. (4) For example, collector's calling hours are restricted. (5) They cannot contact you very early in the morning or late at night. (6) Collectors cannot threaten to seize your property unless its collateral for a loan.

1. Sentence 1: **If you've had problems paying bills, you may be the recipient of a collection agencys' attention.**

   Which correction should be made to sentence 1?

   (1) change <u>you've</u> to <u>youv'e</u>
   (2) change <u>you've</u> to <u>youve'</u>
   (3) change <u>bills</u> to <u>bill's</u>
   (4) change <u>agencys'</u> to <u>agency's</u>
   (5) change <u>agencys'</u> to <u>agencies'</u>

2. Sentence 2: **In the past, such agencies were'nt regulated by law, and they often harassed people.**

   Which correction should be made to sentence 2?

   (1) change <u>agencies</u> to <u>agencies'</u>
   (2) change <u>agencies</u> to <u>agency's</u>
   (3) change <u>were'nt</u> to <u>weren't</u>
   (4) change <u>were'nt</u> to <u>wer'ent</u>
   (5) change <u>were'nt</u> to <u>we'rent</u>

3. Sentence 3: **For that reason, the government has told these agencies what theyre allowed to do.**

   Which correction should be made to sentence 3?

   (1) change <u>theyre</u> to <u>theyr'e</u>
   (2) change <u>theyre</u> to <u>they're</u>
   (3) change <u>theyre</u> to <u>their</u>
   (4) change <u>theyre</u> to <u>theyre are</u>
   (5) no correction is necessary

4. Sentence 4: **For example, collector's calling hours are restricted.**

   Which correction should be made to sentence 4?

   (1) change <u>collector's</u> to <u>collectors'</u>
   (2) change <u>collector's</u> to <u>collectors</u>
   (3) change <u>hours</u> to <u>hour's</u>
   (4) change <u>hours</u> to <u>hours'</u>
   (5) no correction is necessary

5. Sentence 6: **Collectors cannot threaten to seize your property unless its collateral for a loan.**

   Which correction should be made to sentence 6?

   (1) change <u>collectors</u> to <u>collectors'</u>
   (2) change <u>collectors</u> to <u>collector's</u>
   (3) change <u>its</u> to <u>isn't</u>
   (4) change <u>its</u> to <u>its'</u>
   (5) change <u>its</u> to <u>it's</u>

Questions 6 through 9 refer to the following paragraph.

(1) For an increasing number of workers, a day's work wont mean a 9-to-5 job. (2) As one professor of economics stated, "Our's is becoming a 24-hour-a-day economy, seven days a week." (3) Jobs in nursing, sales, and food service are expected to increase, and these job's hours generally include night and weekend shifts. (4) Moreover, many of these jobs have traditionally been womens' jobs. (5) The trend's effect on families remains to be seen.

6. Sentence 1: **For an increasing number of <u>workers, a day's work wont</u> mean a 9-to-5 job.**

Which is the <u>best</u> way to write the underlined portion of this sentence? If the original is the best way, choose option (1).

(1) workers, a day's work wont
(2) worker's, a day's work wont
(3) workers, a day's work won't
(4) workers, a day's work wo'nt
(5) workers, a days work wont

7. Sentence 2: **As one professor of economics stated, "Our's is becoming a 24-hour-a-day economy, seven days a week."**

Which correction should be made to sentence 2?

(1) change <u>economics</u> to <u>economic's</u>
(2) change <u>economics</u> to <u>economics'</u>
(3) change <u>Our's</u> to <u>Ours</u>
(4) change <u>Our's</u> to <u>Ours'</u>
(5) change <u>days</u> to <u>days'</u>

8. Sentence 3: **Jobs in nursing, sales, and food service are expected to increase, and these job's hours generally include night and weekend shifts.**

Which correction should be made to sentence 3?

(1) change <u>sales</u> to <u>sales'</u>
(2) change <u>job's</u> to <u>jobs'</u>
(3) change <u>hours</u> to <u>hour's</u>
(4) change <u>hours</u> to <u>hours'</u>
(5) change <u>shifts</u> to <u>shift's</u>

9. Sentence 4: **Moreover, many of these positions have traditionally been womens' jobs.**

Which correction should be made to sentence 4?

(1) change <u>positions</u> to <u>position's</u>
(2) change <u>womens'</u> to <u>women's</u>
(3) change <u>womens'</u> to <u>womens</u>
(4) change <u>jobs</u> to <u>job's</u>
(5) change <u>jobs</u> to <u>jobs'</u>

[**TIP**]

Possessive pronouns, such as *ours, hers, theirs,* and *its* do show possession, but they do not require apostrophes. If you're unsure about whether *its* needs an apostrophe, read the sentence with *it is* in place of *its.* If the sentence makes sense with *it is,* you may use the contraction *it's,* with an apostrophe. If the sentence does *not* make sense with *it is,* you need the possessive pronoun *its.*

Answers and explanations start on page 116.

Skill 13

Commas in Sentences

On the GED Writing Test, you may see questions about commas in sentences.

Commas in Compound Sentences

In a **compound sentence,** a connecting word joins two **independent clauses.** The connecting words are *and, but, or, nor, for, so,* or *yet.* A comma should be inserted before the connecting word that joins the independent clauses.

Examples: High-speed trains are common in Europe, but the U.S. only has one.

I have never traveled by train, nor have I traveled by air.

In some sentences, the connecting words *and, but, or, nor, for, so,* and *yet* connect two **nouns** or two **verbs** or two **adjectives.** In cases with only two words being connected, a comma is not needed.

Examples: Rail and air travel are both expensive.

Our seats on the plane were soft but cramped.

Commas in Complex Sentences

A **complex sentence** has an **independent clause** and a **dependent clause.** The dependent clause has a subject and a verb, but it is not a complete thought. When a dependent clause begins a sentence, use a comma to separate the clauses.

Dependent clause first: Whether you drive a car or a truck, gas prices are increasing.

When a dependent clause ends a sentence, do *not* use a comma to seperate the clauses.

Dependent clause last: Gas prices are increasing whether you drive a car or a truck.

Read the sentence below. Choose the one best answer to the question.

I hurt my back yesterday so I will not be able to lift anything at work today.

QUESTION: Which correction should be made to this sentence?

(1) insert a comma after back
(2) insert a comma after yesterday
(3) insert a comma after so
(4) insert a comma after able
(5) insert a comma after anything

EXPLANATIONS

(1) No. Inserting a comma after *back* only interrupts the first independent clause rather than joining the two clauses.
(2) **Yes. A comma should be inserted before** *so,* **the connecting word that joins the two independent clauses.**
(3) No. A comma should be inserted before, not after, the connecting word that joins two independent clauses.
(4) No. Inserting a comma after *able* would interrupt the second independent clause and would not make sense in the context of the sentence.
(5) No. Inserting a comma after *anything* would unnecessarily interrupt the second independent clause without separating the two clauses properly.

ANSWER: (2) insert a comma after yesterday

Practice the Skill

(1) The fastest trains in this country run between the capital and New York City but they average only about 80 miles per hour. (2) Because smaller towns have no air service our country needs a system of high-speed trains to connect these towns. (3) Train systems do exist, but they are not always cost efficient or timely. (4) For quick cross-country travel, trains are not the best option.

1. **Sentence 1: The fastest trains in this country run between the capital and New York City but they average only about 80 miles per hour.**

   Which correction should be made to sentence 1?

   (1) insert a comma after <u>country</u>
   (2) insert a comma after <u>between</u>
   (3) insert a comma after <u>capital</u>
   (4) insert a comma after <u>City</u>
   (5) insert a comma after <u>but</u>

   HINT Watch for the connecting words *and, but, or, for, nor, so,* and *yet.* When you see a connecting word, see if it joins two independent clauses. If it does, you know you need a comma *before* the connecting word.

2. **Sentence 2: Because smaller towns have no air <u>service our country needs</u> a system of high-speed trains to connect these towns.**

   What is the <u>best</u> way to write the underlined portion of this sentence? If the original is the best way, choose option (1).

   (1) service our country needs
   (2) service, our country needs
   (3) service our country, needs
   (4) service. Our country needs
   (5) service our country needs,

   HINT Remember that when a dependent clause begins a complex sentence, a comma must be used to separate it from the independent clause.

Answers and Explanations

1. (4) insert a comma after <u>City</u>
Option (4) correctly places a comma at the end of the first independent clause and before the connecting word *but.*

Options (1) and (2) incorrectly suggest placing a comma in the middle of the first independent clause. Option (3) incorrectly uses a comma to separate two nouns joined by *and.* Option (5) incorrectly places the comma after the connecting word *but* instead of before it.

2. (2) service, our country needs
Option (2) correctly places a comma at the end of the dependent clause to separate it from the independent clause in this complex sentence.

Option (1) is not correct because it lacks a comma to separate the dependent clause that begins the sentence from the independent clause that follows. Options (3) and (5) incorrectly suggest placing a comma in the middle of the independent clause. Option (4) is incorrect because dividing the sentence into two sentences will make the dependent clause an incomplete sentence.

Commas in Sentences

Directions: Choose the one best answer to each question.

Questions 1 through 5 refer to the following paragraph.

(1) A good resumé is important in a job search but a good cover letter is just as important. (2) The main points of a resumé are your work history, and your education. (3) Your cover letter should show how you would personally fit in with the new company, and it should briefly highlight your key accomplishments. (4) For example, large organizations rely on teamwork so a letter to such an organization should give at least one example of how you work well with others. (5) When responding to a want ad, address how you are qualified, to meet each job requirement.

1. Sentence 1: **A good resumé is important in a job search but a good cover letter is just as important.**

   Which correction should be made to sentence 1?

   (1) insert a comma after resumé
   (2) insert a comma after important
   (3) insert a comma after search
   (4) insert a comma after but
   (5) insert a comma after letter

2. Sentence 2: **The main points of a resumé are your work history, and your education.**

   What is the best way to write the underlined portion of this sentence? If the original is the best way, choose option (1).

   (1) resumé are your work history, and your
   (2) resumé are your work history and your
   (3) resumé, are your work history and your
   (4) resumé are, your work history and your
   (5) resumé are your work history and, your

3. Sentence 3: **Your cover letter should show how you would personally fit in with the new company, and it should briefly highlight your key accomplishments.**

   What is the best way to write the underlined portion of this sentence? If the original is the best way, choose option (1).

   (1) would personally fit in with the new company, and
   (2) would personally fit in with the new company and
   (3) would, personally fit in with the new company and
   (4) would personally, fit in with the new company and
   (5) would personally fit in with the new company and,

4. Sentence 4: **For example, large organizations rely on teamwork so a letter to such an organization should give at least one example of how you work well with others.**

   Which correction should be made to sentence 4?

   (1) insert a comma after teamwork
   (2) insert a comma after so
   (3) insert a comma after such
   (4) insert a comma after give
   (5) insert a comma after well

5. Sentence 5: **When responding to a want ad, address how you are qualified, to meet each job requirement.**

   Which correction should be made to sentence 5?

   (1) insert a comma after responding
   (2) remove the comma after ad
   (3) insert a comma after address and remove the comma after qualified
   (4) remove the comma after qualified
   (5) remove the comma after qualified and insert a comma after meet

Questions 6 through 9 refer to the following paragraph.

(1) Many people cash their paychecks or government checks at a check-cashing store and they pay high fees to do so. (2) Because, these people do not have checking accounts they cannot take advantage of the benefits of such an account. (3) A checking account keeps money safe in a bank. (4) The account holder makes purchases and pays bills by writing checks, instead of paying with cash. (5) The bank subtracts the amount of each check from the total amount in the account. (6) Though checks are easy to use many people now prefer debit cards. (7) A debit card automatically subtracts the amount of a purchase from the account at the time of purchase.

6. Sentence 1: **Many people cash their paychecks or government checks at a check-cashing store and they pay high fees to do so.**

Which correction should be made to sentence 1?

(1) insert a comma after <u>people</u>
(2) insert a comma after <u>paychecks</u>
(3) insert a comma after <u>or</u>
(4) insert a comma after <u>checks</u>
(5) insert a comma after <u>store</u>

7. Sentence 2: <u>**Because, these people do not have checking accounts they**</u> **cannot take advantage of the benefits of such an account.**

What is the <u>best</u> way to write the underlined portion of this sentence? If the original is the best way, choose option (1).

(1) Because, these people do not have checking accounts they
(2) Because these people, do not have checking accounts they
(3) Because these people do not have, checking accounts they
(4) Because these people do not have checking accounts, they
(5) Because these people do not have checking accounts they

8. Sentence 4: **The account holder makes purchases and pays bills by writing checks, instead of paying with cash.**

What is the <u>best</u> way to write the underlined portion of this sentence? If the original is the best way, choose option (1).

(1) purchases and pays bills by writing checks, instead of
(2) purchases and pays bills by writing checks instead of
(3) purchases, and pays bills by writing checks instead of
(4) purchases and pays bills, by writing checks instead of
(5) purchases and pays bills by writing checks instead, of

9. Sentence 6: **Though checks are easy to use many people now prefer debit cards.**

Which correction should be made to sentence 6?

(1) insert a comma after <u>Though</u>
(2) insert a comma after <u>checks</u>
(3) insert a comma after <u>use</u>
(4) insert a comma after <u>many</u>
(5) insert a comma after <u>people</u>

TIP

Learn how to recognize dependent clauses. They may begin with words such as *after, although, as long as, as soon as, before, because, even though, instead, if, once, since, though, unless, until, when, whether,* and *while.* When you can identify a dependent clause at the beginning of a sentence, you will know it needs a comma to separate it from the independent clause.

Answers and explanations start on page 117.

Skill 14

Unnecessary Commas

On the GED Writing Test, you may see questions about the use of unnecessary commas in sentences.

Do not use a comma to separate pairs of items, such as two nouns, two verbs, or two adjectives.

Examples: Ticket <u>agents</u> and flight <u>attendants</u> hear many complaints from travelers who are unhappy about their flight.

Too often, commercial airlines <u>overbook</u> flights and <u>lose</u> luggage.

Flights that are <u>overcrowded</u> and <u>late</u> do not make for happy travelers.

You will not usually need to use a comma to separate a subject and a verb in a sentence. Sometimes there are many words between a subject and a verb. Read these types of sentences carefully to determine if a comma is needed or if it is unnecessary.

Example: <u>A bag</u> that is routed to the wrong city <u>can ruin</u> an entire vacation.

Do not use a comma after the last item in a series.

Example: Passengers are upset about the crowded parking lots, long lines, and <u>security restrictions</u> that are common in today's airports.

Read the sentence below. Choose the <u>one best answer</u> to the question.

Packing a single suitcase for an extended trip, is a challenge.

QUESTION: Which correction should be made to this sentence?

(1) insert a comma after <u>Packing</u>
(2) insert a comma after <u>single</u>
(3) insert a comma after <u>suitcase</u>
(4) remove the comma after <u>trip</u>
(5) no correction is necessary

EXPLANATIONS

(1) No. A comma after *Packing* would incorrectly interrupt the gerund phrase *Packing a single suitcase*.
(2) No. This option incorrectly separates an adjective from the noun it describes with a comma.
(3) No. A comma after *suitcase* would be unnecessary.
(4) **Yes. Though there are many words between the subject and the verb of this sentence, a comma before the verb is not necessary.**
(5) No. The original sentence contains an unnecessary comma before the verb and needs to be corrected.

ANSWER: (4) remove the comma after <u>trip</u>

Practice the Skill

Try these sample questions. Choose the one best answer to each question. Then check your answers and read the explanations.

(1) When was the last time you boarded an airplane, relaxed in your seat, and had fun, during a flight? (2) My last flight departed a half-hour late and encountered severe weather. (3) A setting that includes stale air and inedible food, offers little glamour or excitement. (4) The person next tp me had a cold and was continually sneezing. (5) A baby at the back of the plane was unhappy and cried during the entire flight. (6) I spilled my drink in my lap and left my book at the terminal. (7) When the flight was over, I was happy to be back home.

1. Sentence 1: **When was the last time you boarded an airplane, relaxed in your seat, and had fun, during a flight?**

Which correction should be made to sentence 1?

(1) remove the comma after <u>airplane</u>
(2) insert a comma after <u>relaxed</u>
(3) remove the comma after <u>seat</u>
(4) insert a comma after <u>and</u>
(5) remove the comma after <u>fun</u>

HINT The items in a list may be single words or may be phrases. When a sentence includes a list, identify each separate item in the series. A comma should follow each item in the series *except* for the last item.

2. Sentence 3: **A setting that includes stale air and inedible food, offers little glamour or excitement.**

Which correction should be made to sentence 3?

(1) insert a comma after <u>setting</u>
(2) insert a comma after <u>includes</u>
(3) insert a comma after <u>air</u>
(4) remove the comma after <u>food</u>
(5) insert a comma after <u>glamour</u>

HINT Identify the subject and the verb in any sentence. Keep in mind that the subject and verb are not usually separated by unnecessary commas.

Answers and Explanations

1. (5) remove the comma after <u>fun</u>
Option (5) correctly removes the comma after *fun*, which is the last item in a series and does not require a comma.

Option (1) incorrectly removes a necessary comma after the first item in the series (*boarded an airplane*). Option (2) is not correct because it inserts an unnecessary comma in the middle of the second item in the series (*relaxed in your seat*). Option (3) incorrectly removes a necessary comma after the second item in the series (*relaxed in your seat*). Option (4) incorrectly inserts a comma after the final item in the series (*had fun*).

2. (4) remove the comma after <u>food</u>
Option (4) correctly removes the unneeded comma that separates the subject from the verb, *offers*.

Options (1) and (2) suggest inserting unnecessary commas between the subject (*setting*) and verb (*offers*). The comma in option (3) is unnecessary; it separates two nouns joined by *and*. The comma in option (5) is unnecessary; it separates two nouns joined by the conjunction *or*.

Unnecessary Commas

Directions: Choose the one best answer to each question.

Questions 1 through 5 refer to the following paragraph.

(1) Many of us accumulate things, and find it hard to throw anything away. (2) As a result, old clothes, empty boxes, never-read magazines, and just plain junk, pile up in our homes until there's clutter everywhere. (3) The solution is to go through your home from top to bottom and to decide what is really necessary. (4) Two or three empty gift boxes might be handy to keep, but ten or twelve, are not. (5) Recycle, throw away, or give unnecessary items to friends, family, or a charity.

1. Sentence 1: **Many of us accumulate things, and find it hard to throw anything away.**

   Which correction should be made to sentence 1?

   (1) insert a comma after <u>us</u>
   (2) insert a comma after <u>accumulate</u> and remove the comma after <u>things</u>
   (3) remove the comma after <u>things</u>
   (4) insert a comma after <u>and</u>
   (5) insert a comma after <u>hard</u>

2. Sentence 2: **As a result, old clothes, empty boxes, never-read magazines, and just plain junk, pile up in our homes until there's clutter everywhere.**

   Which correction should be made to sentence 2?

   (1) remove the comma after <u>clothes</u>
   (2) remove the comma after <u>boxes</u>
   (3) remove the comma after <u>magazines</u>
   (4) remove the comma after <u>junk</u>
   (5) no correction is necessary

3. Sentence 3: **The solution is to go <u>through your home from top to bottom and to decide</u> what is really necessary.**

   Which is the <u>best</u> way to write the underlined portion of this sentence? If the original is the best way, choose option (1).

   (1) through your home from top to bottom and to decide
   (2) through, your home from top to bottom and to decide
   (3) through your home, from top to bottom and to decide
   (4) through your home from top to bottom, and to decide
   (5) through your home from top to bottom and to decide,

4. Sentence 4: **Two or three empty gift boxes might be handy to keep, but ten or twelve, are not.**

   Which correction should be made to sentence 4?

   (1) insert a comma after <u>boxes</u>
   (2) insert a comma after <u>handy</u>
   (3) remove the comma after <u>keep</u>
   (4) insert a comma after <u>ten</u>
   (5) remove the comma after <u>twelve</u>

5. Sentence 5: **Recycle, throw away, or give unnecessary items to friends, family, or a charity.**

   Which correction should be made to sentence 5?

   (1) remove the comma after <u>recycle</u>
   (2) remove the comma after <u>away</u>
   (3) remove the comma after <u>friends</u>
   (4) remove the comma after <u>family</u>
   (5) no correction is necessary

Questions 6 through 10 refer to the following paragraph.

(1) Your house or apartment, can be kept free from clutter if you simply acquire a few good habits. (2) Suppose you buy a new sweater or shirt. (3) Then give an old sweater or shirt away. (4) Go through your closets, and dressers once a year, and get rid of anything you haven't worn since the last cleanup. (5) Designate a collection spot for old or outgrown magazines, books, toys, and clothes. (6) When an organization such as Goodwill calls, and asks for donations, you'll have things ready. (7) Your home, and your life will be the better for it. (8) A clutter-free home will lead to a clutter-free life.

6. Sentence 1: **Your house or apartment, can be kept free from clutter if you simply acquire a few good habits.**

Which correction should be made to sentence 1?

(1) insert a comma after <u>house</u>
(2) remove the comma after <u>apartment</u>
(3) insert a comma after <u>clutter</u>
(4) insert a comma after <u>acquire</u>
(5) insert a comma after <u>few</u>

7. Sentence 4: **Go through your <u>closets, and dressers once a year,</u> and get rid of anything you haven't worn since the last cleanup.**

Which is the <u>best</u> way to write the underlined portion of this sentence? If the original is the best way, choose option (1).

(1) closets, and dressers once a year,
(2) closets, and dressers, once a year,
(3) closets and dressers, once a year,
(4) closets and dressers once a year,
(5) closets and dressers once, a year

8. Sentence 6: **When an organization such as Goodwill calls, and asks for donations, you'll have things ready.**

Which correction should be made to sentence 6?

(1) insert a comma after <u>organization</u>
(2) insert a comma after <u>Goodwill</u>
(3) remove the comma after <u>calls</u>
(4) remove the comma after <u>donations</u>
(5) insert a comma after <u>you'll</u>

9. Sentence 7: **<u>Your home, and your life</u> will be the better for it.**

Which is the <u>best</u> way to write the underlined portion of this sentence? If the original is the best way, choose option (1).

(1) Your home, and your life
(2) Your home and your life
(3) Your home, and your, life
(4) Your, home and your life
(5) Your, home and your life,

10. Sentence 8: **A clutter-free <u>home will lead to a</u> clutter-free life.**

Which is the <u>best</u> way to rewrite the underlined portion of this sentence? If the original is the best way, choose option (1).

(1) home will lead to a
(2) home will, lead to a
(3) home, will lead to a
(4) home. Will lead to a
(5) home will lead, to a

> **TIP**
>
> Be aware that some sentences include pairs of words, such as two nouns or two verbs. Pairs of nouns or verbs that are joined by *and*, *but*, or *or* should not be separated by a comma. When three or more nouns or verbs are joined, you will need to separate them using a comma.

Answers and explanations start on page 117.

Spelling Homonyms

Some questions on the GED Writing Test may ask you about the spelling of words. Many spelling errors occur because of confusion among **homonyms.** Homonyms are words that sound alike but have different spellings and different meanings. For example, in the sentence "Workers' energy levels are often weak by the end of the week," *weak* and *week* sound the same, but clearly have two different spellings and different meanings, which means they are homonyms. Here are some examples of other homonyms.

- already (previously)
  all ready (completely ready)
- board (a flat piece of wood or other material)
  bored (uninterested)
- coarse (rough, textured)
  course (a path or track)
- council (a group)
  counsel (advice; to advise)
- peace (a state of calm)
  piece (a part or portion)

- principal (most important; the head of a school)
  principle (an important rule)
- role (the function of something; a part played by an actor)
  roll (a type of bread; to turn over)
- stationary (not moving)
  stationery (writing paper)
- to (in that direction)
  too (in addition)
  two (a number that is more than one, less than three)

Some possessive pronouns and contractions, like homonyms, sound alike but are spelled differently. These include *its*, the pronoun, and *it's*, the contraction for *it is; your*, the pronoun, and *you're*, the contraction for *you are; their*, the pronoun, and *they're*, the contraction for *they are*; and *whose*, the pronoun, and *who's*, the contraction for *who is*. Finally, in addition to *their* and *they're*, *there* means "in that place."

Read the sentence below. Choose the <u>one best answer</u> to the question.

If you're in a meeting at work and feel board, it's important not to let it show.

QUESTION: Which correction should be made to this sentence?

(1) replace <u>you're</u> with <u>your</u>
(2) replace <u>in</u> with <u>inn</u>
(3) replace <u>board</u> with <u>bored</u>
(4) replace <u>it's</u> with <u>its</u>
(5) replace <u>to</u> with <u>too</u>

EXPLANATIONS

(1) No. The sentence is correct with *you're*, the contraction for *you are*.
(2) No. The sentence is correct with the preposition *in*. An *inn* is a type of hotel.
(3) **Yes. The meaning of the sentence indicates that the word should be *bored*, meaning "uninterested." A *board* is a flat piece of wood.**
(4) No. The sentence is correct with *it's*, the contraction for *it is*.
(5) No. The sentence is correct with *to*, which is part of the verb *to let. Too*, meaning "in addition," would not make sense in the sentence.

ANSWER: (3) replace <u>board</u> with <u>bored</u>

Practice the Skill

Try these sample questions. Choose the <u>one best answer</u> to each question. Then check your answers and read the explanations.

(1) Its known by many people that Friday is the worst day of the week to call a business meeting. (2) By that day, I no that I may be bored, tired, or thinking of the upcoming weekend. (3) Workers watch the clock inch slowly toward quitting time. (4) Everyone is ready for a little time off.

1. Sentence 1: **Its known by many people that Friday is the worst day of the week to call a business meeting.**

   Which correction should be made to sentence 1?

   (1) replace <u>Its</u> with <u>It's</u>
   (2) replace <u>by</u> with <u>buy</u>
   (3) replace <u>week</u> with <u>weak</u>
   (4) replace <u>to</u> with <u>two</u>
   (5) no correction is necessary

   HINT Confusing *its* and *it's* is a common error. Test the word by reading the sentence with *it is* in place of the word in the sentence. If the sentence makes sense that way, *it's* is the correct choice. If the sentence doesn't make sense that way, use the word *its*.

2. Sentence 2: **By that day, I no that I may be bored, tired, or thinking of the upcoming weekend.**

   Which correction should be made to sentence 2?

   (1) replace <u>By</u> with <u>Buy</u>
   (2) replace <u>no</u> with <u>know</u>
   (3) replace <u>be</u> with <u>bee</u>
   (4) replace <u>bored</u> with <u>board</u>
   (5) replace <u>or</u> with <u>ore</u>

   HINT Many frequently used words, such as *no, by, be,* and *or,* are homonyms. It is important to learn these words to avoid frequent spelling errors.

Answers and Explanations

1. (1) replace <u>Its</u> with <u>It's</u>
Option (1) corrects the spelling error by replacing *Its* with *It's*, the contraction of *it is*, which makes sense in the sentence.

Option (2) incorrectly replaces the preposition *by* with the verb *buy*, but it does not make sense to have a verb in that part of the sentence. Option (3) replaces the noun *week* with the adjective *weak*, which does not make sense because nothing in the sentence is being described as *weak*. Option (4) replaces the preposition *to* with the number *two*, which does not make sense. Option (5), the original sentence, incorrectly uses the possessive pronoun *Its* where the contraction for *It is,* or *It's,* is needed.

2. (2) replace <u>no</u> with <u>know</u>
Option (2) correctly replaces the negative word *no* with the verb *know*, which is needed to give the sentence a complete and correct meaning.

Option (1) is not correct because it replaces the preposition *By* with the verb *Buy*, meaning "to purchase something," which does not make sense since you cannot *purchase that day*. Option (3) incorrectly replaces the verb *be* with the noun *bee*, which is the name of an insect and does not make sense in this sentence. Option (4) incorrectly replaces the adjective *bored* with the noun *board*, referring to a flat piece of wood, which does not make sense in the context of the sentence. Option (5) is not correct because it replaces the conjunction *or* with the noun *ore*. Ore is a mineral or rock that can be mined as a source of metal, and that word does not belong in the sentence.

Spelling Homonyms

Directions: Choose the <u>one best answer</u> to each question.

<u>Questions 1 through 5</u> refer to the following paragraph.

(1) Excess weight can lessen your chances four a healthy life and can increase your chances of heart disease. (2) How do you know if you're at risk or not? (3) There is a simple weigh to determine whether your weight puts you at a greater risk factor for heart disease. (4) First, get a tape measure and measure your waist and hips. (5) For a man, doctors say the waste should be no larger than the hips. (6) For a woman whose in her child-bearing years, doctors recommend that the waist not be greater than 80 percent of the hip measurement. (7) If a person's measurements due result in a number greater than those described, it's never too late to begin a diet and exercise program that will play a role in reducing the risk of heart disease.

1. Sentence 1: **Excess weight can lessen your chances four a healthy life and can increase your chances of heart disease.**

   Which correction should be made to sentence 1?

   (1) replace <u>lessen</u> with <u>lesson</u>
   (2) replace <u>your</u> with <u>you're</u>
   (3) replace <u>four</u> with <u>for</u>
   (4) replace <u>heart</u> with <u>hart</u>
   (5) no correction is necessary

2. Sentence 2: **How do you know if you're at risk or not?**

   Which correction should be made to sentence 2?

   (1) replace <u>do</u> with <u>due</u>
   (2) replace <u>know</u> with <u>no</u>
   (3) replace <u>you're</u> with <u>your</u>
   (4) replace <u>not</u> with <u>knot</u>
   (5) no correction is necessary

3. Sentence 3: **There is a simple weigh to determine whether your weight puts you at a greater risk factor for heart disease.**

   Which correction should be made to sentence 3?

   (1) replace <u>There</u> with <u>They're</u>
   (2) replace <u>weigh</u> with <u>way</u>
   (3) replace <u>for</u> with <u>four</u>
   (4) replace <u>whether</u> with <u>weather</u>
   (5) replace <u>your</u> with <u>you're</u>

4. Sentence 6: **For a woman whose in her child-bearing years, doctors recommend that the waist not be greater than 80 percent of the hip measurement.**

   Which correction should be made to sentence 6?

   (1) replace <u>For</u> with <u>Four</u>
   (2) replace <u>whose</u> with <u>who's</u>
   (3) replace <u>waist</u> with <u>waste</u>
   (4) replace <u>be</u> with <u>bee</u>
   (5) replace <u>greater</u> with <u>grater</u>

5. Sentence 7: **If a person's measurements due result in a number greater than those described, it's never too late to begin a diet and exercise program that will play a role in reducing the risk of heart disease.**

   Which correction should be made to sentence 7?

   (1) replace <u>due</u> with <u>do</u>
   (2) replace <u>role</u> with <u>roll</u>
   (3) replace <u>it's</u> with <u>its</u>
   (4) replace <u>too</u> with <u>two</u>
   (5) replace <u>in</u> with <u>inn</u>

Questions 6 through 9 refer to this paragraph.

(1) You may or may not know that local weather forecasters used to accomplish there task with a few simple instruments, such as wind vanes and barometers. (2) Today's forecaster is equipped with computers, radar, and satellites to map and predict the weather. (3) Perhaps this is why there are such detailed computer graphics in the weather segment we sea each night. (4) However, many people aren't interested in learning about stationary fronts, jet streams, or whether a peace of Alaska is going to break a snowfall record today. (5) They simply want good counsel about whether its going to rain or shine and whether they should wear a jacket.

6. Sentence 1: **You may or may not know that local weather forecasters used to accomplish there task with a few simple instruments, such as wind vanes and barometers.**

Which correction should be made to sentence 1?

(1) replace or with ore
(2) replace not with knot
(3) replace weather with whether
(4) replace there with their
(5) replace vanes with veins

7. Sentence 3: **Perhaps this is why there are such detailed computer graphics in the weather segment we sea each night.**

Which correction should be made to sentence 3?

(1) replace in with inn
(2) replace we with wee
(3) replace sea with see
(4) replace night with knight
(5) replace there with they're

8. Sentence 4: **However, many people aren't interested in learning about stationary fronts, jet streams, or whether a peace of Alaska is going to break a snowfall record today.**

Which correction should be made to sentence 4?

(1) replace stationary with stationery
(2) replace or with ore
(3) replace whether with weather
(4) replace peace with piece
(5) replace break with brake

9. Sentence 5: **They simply want good counsel about whether its going to rain or shine and whether they should wear a jacket.**

Which correction should be made to sentence 5?

(1) replace counsel with council
(2) replace whether with weather
(3) replace its with it's
(4) replace to with too
(5) replace rain with reign

Answers and explanations start on page 118.

TIP

Confusing *their*, *there*, and *they're* is a common mistake. Here are some tips to help you choose the right word:
- *There* often refers to situations or conditions, and a form of the verb *to be* (is, are, will be, can be) usually closely follows this word.
- *Their* is a possessive pronoun. It shows ownership. A noun telling what is owned (the object) will closely follow the word *their*.
- *They're* is a contraction of *they are*. A verb ending in *-ing* or an adjective generally follows the contraction *they're*.

KEY Skill 16

Topic Sentences

On the GED Writing Test, you may see questions about **topic sentences.** The topic sentence states the **main idea** of a paragraph. A well-written topic sentence lets readers know what the subject of the paragraph will be. The other sentences support the topic sentence by giving examples or details that tell more about the subject. The topic sentence may appear anywhere in a paragraph; however, it is usually the first sentence of a paragraph.

A good topic sentence is specific, not vague. It states the main point of the paragraph clearly.

Poor example: To find the right apartment, you should consider some very important things.

Good example: To find the right apartment, you should consider three important qualities—location, price, and suitability.

A good topic sentence also lets readers know what to expect in the paragraph.

Poor example: Research shows that using cell phones while driving can be dangerous.

Good example: Research shows that using cell phones while driving is an increasing cause of serious accidents.

Read the paragraph below. Choose the <u>one best answer</u> to the question.

Board games are a great way to pass the time for adults and children. You probably have some that you haven't played for a while. Looking through old photo albums is another enjoyable activity. The pictures might remind you of great stories to tell your children about years past. Working on crafts together can also be fun. Even if you're low on craft supplies, you probably have scissors, glue, and paper or old magazines. With just these simple materials and tools, you and the kids can make collages.

QUESTION: Which of the following would be the best topic sentence if inserted at the beginning of the paragraph?

(1) Here's what to do on a rainy day.
(2) Every summer has at least a few rainy days.
(3) Children often do not know what to do on a rainy day.
(4) There are many activities you can do with children on a rainy day.
(5) No correction is necessary.

EXPLANATIONS

(1) No. This option is too vague about the topic of the paragraph.
(2) No. This option does not introduce the topic of the paragraph.
(3) No. This option does not clearly state the main point of the paragraph.
(4) **Yes. This option states the main point and lets readers know specifically what to expect in the paragraph.**
(5) No. The paragraph needs a topic sentence that states its main point.

ANSWER: (4) There are many activities you can do with children on a rainy day.

Practice the Skill

Try these sample questions. Choose the <u>one best answer</u> to each question. Then check your answers and read the explanations.

(1) It can take anywhere from a week to a month or more to prepare for a move. (2) The move itself can take a day or a week, depending on the distance of the move. (3) Unpacking can sometimes last for months after the move. (4) The more organized you are from the beginning, however, the less time it will take for you to settle into your new home.

(5) First, locate the nearest hospital or emergency clinic, and be sure you know how to get there. (6) Next, telephone the Department of Motor Vehicles and inquire about the procedure for acquiring a new license. (7) Then check on voter registration rules because a residency period may be required before you can vote in your new location.

1. Which topic sentence would be most effective if inserted at the beginning of the first paragraph?

   (1) People move to a new home for many different reasons.
   (2) It is best to be prepared for a large task.
   (3) Moving takes hard work and lots of organization.
   (4) Be sure to have plenty of boxes and packing tape on hand if you are getting ready to move.
   (5) The time it takes to move can depend on how far you are moving.

   HINT A good topic sentence clearly tells readers what to expect in the paragraph.

2. Which topic sentence would be most effective if inserted at the beginning of the second paragraph?

   (1) Before you begin any new tasks, you should be congratulated for all of your hard work.
   (2) To help you get settled after the move, you should complete a few essential tasks as soon as possible.
   (3) Many things remain to be done.
   (4) Here is your new "to do" list.
   (5) No correction is necessary.

   HINT Determine what all of the details in the paragraph are about when selecting a topic sentence for the paragraph.

Answers and Explanations

1. (3) Moving takes hard work and lots of organization.
Option (3) suggests a sentence that clearly introduces the main topic of the paragraph and hints at what is to follow.

Option (1) would not effectively begin the paragraph because the paragraph is not about why people move. Option (2) is vague; it does not identify the nature of the "large task." Option (4) does not clearly tell readers what to expect in the paragraph. Option (5) repeats one detail from the paragraph instead of introducing its topic.

2. (2) To help you get settled after the move, you should complete a few essential tasks as soon as possible.
Option (2) clearly tells readers that the paragraph will be about tasks to do after moving to a new community.

Option (1) does not relate to the specific content of the paragraph. Options (3) and (4) are too vague to effectively begin the paragraph. Option (5) is not correct because the paragraph needs a topic sentence that states its main point.

Topic Sentences

Directions: Choose the one best answer to each question.

Questions 1 through 3 refer to the following paragraphs.

(1) A new kind of criminal has appeared—the identity thief. (2) Instead of stealing money, jewels, electronic equipment, or artwork, identity thieves steal numbers and information. (3) They try to get their hands on your name and personal information, such as your social security number. (4) They steal your financial history. (5) They steal your identity.

(6) Identity thieves steal credit card numbers for their own use, running up huge bills. (7) They take out loans under false names and may even buy or sell houses. (8) They also sell identities to fellow thieves, who repeat the cycle. (9) It can take years to undo the damage.

(10) Never give your social security number over the phone or online. (11) Do not have it printed on your checks or let merchants use it for identification. (12) Similarly, guard your credit card numbers carefully. (13) Do not leave receipts behind. (14) Also, some thieves steal mail to look for these numbers, so collect your mail promptly and send your outgoing mail from a post office.

(15) New ways of doing business have created new opportunities for thieves. (16) With today's increasing dependence upon data systems, your financial life could be at risk. (17) Protect your identity carefully. (18) Someone could be watching, waiting to become you.

1. Which sentence would be most effective if inserted at the beginning of the second paragraph (sentences 6–9)?

   (1) What is identity theft?
   (2) This new kind of crime is called identity theft.
   (3) You should protect yourself against identity theft.
   (4) Identity thieves are usually computer experts.
   (5) Identity thieves use stolen information in several ways.

2. Which sentence would be most effective if inserted at the beginning of the third paragraph (sentences 10–14)?

   (1) Your social security number could be a problem.
   (2) There are several things you can do to protect your identity.
   (3) Identity thieves are not like other thieves.
   (4) Do not lend out your credit cards.
   (5) No correction is necessary.

3. Which sentence would be most effective if inserted at the beginning of the fourth paragraph (sentences 15–18)?

   (1) Previous ways of doing business were better.
   (2) If you are careful, you can protect yourself from identity thieves.
   (3) Identity thieves have many ways of obtaining your personal information.
   (4) The more we depend on data systems, the more we are at risk.
   (5) No correction is necessary.

Questions 4 through 6 refer to the following paragraphs.

(1) The JetExpert printer is an inkjet printer intended for the home office. (2) The printer can print in both black-and-white and color. (3) Unlike many printers, the JetExpert has a separate cartridge for each color. (4) You replace only the one that is empty. (5) Waste is thus reduced.

(6) In normal mode, the JetExpert prints black-and-white or color with high resolution. (7) In draft mode, the printer uses less ink and saves money. (8) When used with photo paper and the software on your computer, in photo mode the JetExpert produces photo-shop quality prints. (9) The JetExpert's three printing modes make it one of the most versatile printers on the market.

(10) The larger tray, called the standard paper tray, is located at the bottom of the printer. (11) This tray holds up to 100 sheets of 8.5 x 11-inch paper. (12) The multipurpose tray, located in the center front of the printer, can hold 50 sheets of legal-size paper, or five envelopes. (13) The multipurpose tray is used when the print job involves envelopes, transparency sheets, or labels.

(14) The JetExpert is compatible with any type of computer or operating system. (15) The JetExpert uses USB technology for easy connection. (16) Controls are easy to use, and access to paper and cartridges is a snap. (17) The price is competitive too. (18) Simple to set up, operate, and maintain, the JetExpert is a value-priced printer that provides genuine value.

> **TIP**
>
> Before deciding which sentence is the best topic sentence, read all the supporting details and sentences of the paragraph. Then try to summarize the main idea in one sentence. Ask yourself, "Could a reader predict what the paragraph is about based only on that sentence?"

4. Which of the following sentences is the topic sentence of the first paragraph (sentences 1–5)?

   (1) The JetExpert printer is an inkjet printer intended for the home office.
   (2) The printer can print in both black-and-white and color.
   (3) Unlike many printers, the JetExpert has a separate cartridge for each color.
   (4) You replace only the one that is empty.
   (5) Waste is thus reduced.

5. Which of the following sentences is the topic sentence of the second paragraph (sentences 6–9)?

   (1) In normal mode, the JetExpert prints black-and-white or color with high resolution.
   (2) In draft mode, the printer uses less ink and saves money.
   (3) When used with photo paper and the software on your computer, in photo mode the JetExpert produces photo-shop quality prints.
   (4) The JetExpert's three printing modes make it one of the most versatile printers on the market.
   (5) This paragraph has no topic sentence.

6. Which of the following sentences would be most effective if inserted at the beginning of the third paragraph (sentences 10–13)?

   (1) The JetExpert has a large tray you can easily see.
   (2) The multipurpose tray is a smaller tray.
   (3) The JetExpert printer has two paper trays.
   (4) The JetExpert printer can print almost anything.
   (5) Some printers are difficult to set up and maintain.

Answers and explanations start on page 119.

Skill 17

Transition Words

On the GED Writing Test, you may see questions that ask you to correct faulty transitions. **Transition words** connect the sentences in a paragraph by showing relationships between ideas. Transition words provide a sense of direction to the text and indicate what kind of information will follow the transition.

Example: Mr. Jacobs expects all employees to be on time. <u>In addition</u>, he expects everyone's appearance to be neat and clean.

(Note that a comma follows the underlined transition words in the sentence above.)

Different transition words and phrases show different kinds of relationships. Some show how ideas are connected. Some show that ideas are different from one another.

Transition Words and Phrases	Type of Relationship Indicated
furthermore, in addition, also	addition
therefore, as a result	cause and effect
similarly	comparison
however, on the other hand, in spite of	contrast
specifically, for example, for instance	example
first, second, then, next, finally	sequence
now, meanwhile, since, then, later	time

Read the paragraph below. Choose the <u>one best answer</u> to the question.

(1) Filling in for an absent co-worker can be a challenge. (2) The first step is to clarify exactly what tasks you need to cover. (3) Therefore, pay close attention to telephone calls and e-mails to make sure that urgent matters are taken care of quickly. (4) Finally, keep track of what you do, and let your co-worker know what has been done.

QUESTION: Which correction should be made to sentence 3?

    (1) replace <u>Therefore</u> with <u>Next</u>
    (2) replace <u>Therefore</u> with <u>However</u>
    (3) replace <u>Therefore</u> with <u>First</u>
    (4) replace <u>Therefore</u> with <u>As a result</u>
    (5) replace <u>Therefore</u> with <u>On the other hand</u>

EXPLANATIONS

    (1) **Yes. The words *first* in sentence 2 and *Finally* in sentence 4 clearly establish a sequence. Sentence 3 is part of that sequence, and *Next* is a logical sequence word.**
    (2) No. The transition *However* would indicate contrast, but there is no contrast between the ideas in sentence 3 and the previously expressed ideas.
    (3) No. Sentence 2 identifies the first step, so sentence 3 cannot begin with *First*.
    (4) No. There is no cause-and-effect relationship between sentence 3 and the previous sentence, so *As a result* is not correct.
    (5) No. The transition *On the other hand* would indicate contrast, but there is no contrast between the ideas in sentence 3 and the previously expressed ideas.

ANSWER: (1) replace <u>Therefore</u> with <u>Next</u>

Practice the Skill

(1) I have complete knowledge of the printing process, including the very latest developments in technology. (2) Furthermore, my communication skills have been confirmed through my work with a sometimes-demanding public. (3) However, the workforce realignments that are necessary in our current economy have trained me to handle added responsibilities.

1. Sentence 2: **Furthermore, my communication skills have been confirmed through my work with a sometimes-demanding public.**

Which of the following words or phrases provides a transition?

(1) Furthermore
(2) communication
(3) have been
(4) through
(5) with

HINT Transition words and phrases establish relationships between sentences. Which of the choices shows a relationship between ideas from the previous sentences?

2. Sentence 3: **However, the workforce realignments that are necessary in our current economy have trained me to handle added responsibilities.**

Which correction should be made to sentence 3?

(1) replace <u>However</u> with <u>For example</u>
(2) replace <u>However</u> with <u>Since then</u>
(3) replace <u>However</u> with <u>Later</u>
(4) replace <u>However</u> with <u>In addition</u>
(5) no correction is necessary

HINT Transition words and phrases help readers know the direction the text is going. Determine the relationship between the ideas in two sentences and decide which transition best shows that relationship.

Answers and Explanations

1. (1) Furthermore
Option (1) correctly identifies the transition word in the sentence, which is *Furthermore*.

The choices in options (2), (3), (4), and (5) are not transition words or phrases. Transition words and phrases show a relationship between the ideas in sentences. Option (2) is being used as an adjective to describe the noun *skills*. Option (3) is a verb phrase. Options (4) and (5) are both prepositions, and are not being used to show transitions.

2. (4) replace <u>However</u> with <u>In addition</u>
Option (4) is correct because the transition *In addition* indicates that sentence 3 provides an additional example of the author's skills.

Option (1) is not the best choice because the transition *For example* would inaccurately suggest that sentence 3 supports sentence 2 by presenting an example of how the author's communication skills have been confirmed. Options (2) and (3) suggest sequences in time that do not make sense in the context of the paragraph. Option (5) is not correct because the transition *However* inaccurately suggests that the ideas in sentence 3 contrast with ideas presented earlier.

Transition Words

Directions: Choose the <u>one best answer</u> to each question.

<u>Questions 1 through 7</u> refer to the following instructions.

Changing ID Codes and Passwords

(A)

(1) The *MathPrep* software allows students to use the computer to study for any standardized math test. (2) Students read through each lesson and then the problems related to the complete lessons. (3) Similarly, the program grades students' work and records where they stopped. (4) For security, each user has an identification (ID) code and password that must be typed in correctly before the student can start working. (5) IDs and passwords can have up to 17 characters and can include numbers, letters, and symbols.

(B)

(6) If another student accidentally or intentionally uses your security codes, incorrect information is permanently entered into your record. (7) Such errors cause great confusion for both students and teachers. (8) You should not share your ID or password with any other student. (9) If you think someone else is intentionally using your security codes, change them as soon as possible. (10) IDs and passwords can be changed at any time, and once changed, the original codes are no longer valid.

(C)

Instructions:

(11) If you need to change your ID or password, follow these steps. (12) First, choose *Codes* from the list of security options. (13) As a result, type your new ID in the ID dialog box. (14) Then press the TAB key. (15) Enter your new password in the password box. (16) Click the OK button. (17) It's as easy as that.

(D)

Warnings and reminders:

- (18) Students often press the Enter key after they type in a new code. (19) This is a common mistake. (20) You *must* click the OK button to enter the change in the database. (21) The program will continue to use your original codes.

- (22) To create a secure code, use information that other students would not ordinarily know. (23) Also, choose a code that you can remember without writing it down. (24) For example, other users may not know that Cleopatra is your pet's name. (25) It would, therefore, be a secure code. (26) If *23-55-18* is the combination to a lock that you use every day, you are likely to remember these numbers easily.

(E)

If you forget your codes:

(27) If this happens, ask your teacher for help. (28) Don't get in the habit of relying on teachers to supply your codes. (29) Instructors may not always be available in the classroom.

1. Sentence 3: **Similarly, the program grades students' work and records where they stopped.**

   Which correction should be made to sentence 3?

   (1) replace <u>Similarly</u> with <u>Then</u>
   (2) replace <u>Similarly</u> with <u>However</u>
   (3) replace <u>Similarly</u> with <u>For instance</u>
   (4) replace <u>Similarly</u> with <u>Meanwhile</u>
   (5) no correction is necessary

2. Sentence 8: **You should not share your ID or password with any other student.**

   Which is the most effective rewrite of sentence 8?

   (1) However, you should not share your ID or password with any other student.
   (2) For example, you should not share your ID or password with any other student.
   (3) Second, you should not tell your ID or password to any other student.
   (4) Therefore, you should not share your ID or password with any other student.
   (5) no revision is necessary

3. Sentence 13: **As a result, type your new ID in the ID dialog box.**

   Which correction should be made to sentence 13?

   (1) replace <u>As a result</u> with <u>Similarly</u>
   (2) replace <u>As a result</u> with <u>Next</u>
   (3) replace <u>As a result</u> with <u>For example</u>
   (4) replace <u>As a result</u> with <u>Finally</u>
   (5) no correction is necessary

4. Sentence 16: **Click the OK button.**

   Which is the most effective rewrite of sentence 16?

   (1) In addition, click the OK button.
   (2) As a result, click the OK button.
   (3) Since, click the OK button.
   (4) Finally, click the OK button.
   (5) no correction is necessary

5. Sentence 21: **The program will continue to use your original codes.**

   Which correction should be made to sentence 21?

   (1) replace <u>The program</u> with <u>First, the program</u>
   (2) replace <u>The program</u> with <u>As a result, the program</u>
   (3) replace <u>The program</u> with <u>Otherwise, the program</u>
   (4) replace <u>The program</u> with <u>Now, the program</u>
   (5) no correction is necessary

6. Sentence 23: **Also, choose a code that you can remember without writing it down.**

   Which of the following words or phrases is a transition word in sentence 23?

   (1) Also
   (2) choose
   (3) that
   (4) without
   (5) it down

7. Sentence 28: **Don't get in the habit of relying on teachers to supply your codes.**

   Which correction should be made to sentence 28?

   (1) replace <u>Don't</u> with <u>However, don't</u>
   (2) replace <u>Don't</u> with <u>For instance, don't</u>
   (3) replace <u>Don't</u> with <u>Meanwhile, don't</u>
   (4) replace <u>Don't</u> with <u>First, don't</u>
   (5) replace <u>Don't</u> with <u>Similarly, don't</u>

[**TIP**]

Transition words and phrases indicate the relationship of a sentence with previous sentences. Before you decide on an appropriate transition word for any sentence, review the ideas in previous sentences for context clues.

Answers and explanations start on page 120.

Irrelevant Sentences

An **irrelevant sentence** in a paragraph is one that does not relate to the **topic**, either by providing detail about the topic or by providing a transition to another paragraph. Irrelevant sentences contain unnecessary, personal, or misplaced information.

Unnecessary Information: Sometimes writers include unnecessary information, too much detail, or information not related to the main topic:

> Choosing a cell phone plan can be complicated. There are many plans out there, and none looks quite the same. Cell phones are actually radio transmitters, and they have been around longer than you think. To get the best deal on a cell phone plan, you need to analyze your use.

The sentence *Cell phones are actually radio transmitters, and they have been around longer than you think* takes the paragraph in a confusing direction away from the topic.

Personal Information: Sometimes writers include irrelevant personal information:

> Choosing a cell phone plan can be complicated. There are many plans out there, and none looks quite the same. My first cell phone was a simple one. To get the best deal on a cell phone plan, you need to analyze your use.

The sentence *My first cell phone was a simple one* is irrelevant to the main points.

Misplaced Information: Sometimes writers put information in the wrong place:

> Choosing a cell phone plan can be complicated. There are many plans out there, and none looks quite the same. Phones with lots of features cost more. To get the best deal on a cell phone plan, you need to analyze your use.

The sentence *Phones with lots of features cost more* may be useful elsewhere in an article about cell phone plans, but in this paragraph, it is confusing.

Read the paragraph below. Choose the <u>one best answer</u> to the question.

(1) Bicycling, carpooling, using mass transit, and even good-old-fashioned walking are all forms of alternate transportation. (2) With fuel prices so high, any of these will help save fuel and money. (3) You probably remember when you learned to ride a bike. (4) Unfortunately, these alternatives are most practical in cities. (5) Rural dwellers in most states have fewer options. (6) How might transportation planning include them?

QUESTION: Which revision would improve the effectiveness of this paragraph?

    (1) remove sentence 2
    (2) remove sentence 3
    (3) remove sentence 4
    (4) remove sentence 5
    (5) remove sentence 6

EXPLANATIONS

    (1) No. This sentence develops the topic introduced in sentence 1.
    (2) **Yes. This sentence does not contribute to or develop the main idea.**
    (3) No. This sentence develops an important idea about alternative transportation.
    (4) No. This sentence is relevant; it states a problem related to the topic.
    (5) No. This sentence poses an important question relevant to ideas.

ANSWER: (2) remove sentence 3

Practice the Skill

Try these sample questions. Choose the one best answer to each question. Then check your answers and read the explanations.

(1) Children often want a puppy. (2) It's an understandable desire, and who doesn't love the image of a kid hugging his Sheltie or snuggling her Lab? (3) But before you get carried away and come home with a dog, give some thought to the responsibility you would be undertaking. (4) Your childhood dog probably gave you a lot of great memories. (5) Take stock of how you live. (6) Cast a sharp eye on the abilities of your children. (7) Think about what life will be like for the critter you get.

(8) Depending on the breed of dog, that puppy may live a dozen years or more. (9) The size of the dog is usually related to the purpose for which it was bred. (10) What is your life going to be like for the next decade? (11) If there is no one home during the day, that cute little puppy may turn into Fido the Furniture Eater, or worse. (12) House-training a dog is no easy task and requires a lot of attention and patience. (13) Are you up to it?

1. Which revision would improve the effectiveness of the first paragraph (sentences 1–7)?

    (1) remove sentence 2
    (2) remove sentence 4
    (3) remove sentence 5
    (4) remove sentence 6
    (5) remove sentence 7

    HINT Look for information that seems unnecessary, is personal in a way that distracts rather than adds, or seems to belong elsewhere.

2. Which revision would improve the effectiveness of the second paragraph (sentences 8–13)?

    (1) remove sentence 8
    (2) remove sentence 9
    (3) remove sentence 10
    (4) remove sentence 12
    (5) remove sentence 13

    HINT An irrelevant sentence may seem to change the subject in the middle of a paragraph. Does the information in the sentence relate directly to the rest of the paragraph?

Answers and Explanations

1. (2) remove sentence 4
Option (2) is correct because memories of a childhood dog are not relevant to the decision of whether or not a household can take on the responsibility of pet ownership.

Option (1) is incorrect because sentence 2 is relevant, discussing the genuine appeal of a dog. Options (3), (4), and (5) are not correct because each sentence suggested in these options gives a relevant guideline to evaluating whether to get a dog.

2. (2) remove sentence 9
Option (2) is the best choice because the sentence raises an entirely new topic unrelated to the topic at hand.

Option (1) is incorrect because sentence 8 gives information relevant to considering whether or not a household can take on the responsibility of owning a dog. Option (3) is incorrect because sentence 10 asks a question that directly relates to the idea presented in sentence 8. Option (4) is incorrect because sentence 12 gives information relevant to the topic. Option (5) is incorrect because sentence 13 asks a question that directly relates to sentence 12.

Irrelevant Sentences

Directions: Choose the <u>one best answer</u> to each question.

<u>Questions 1 through 4</u> refer to the following paragraphs.

(1) Something useful for anyone is a small household toolkit. (2) For people who are starting out on their own or who just want to make life easier, a small household toolkit kept close by is a big help. (3) Living on your own for the first time is a big challenge. (4) A small toolkit to grab in a hurry is convenient for the many small jobs that pop up around the home.

(5) Get a box about the size of a small fishing tackle box. (6) It should be about fourteen inches long by eight inches wide.

(7) Stock the toolkit with some basic items. (8) One basic tool to keep on hand is a tack hammer. (9) There is rarely need for a big carpenter's hammer. (10) There are many different kinds of hammers. (11) Add a couple of regular slot screwdrivers of different sizes and a couple of Phillips screwdrivers, the ones with the x-shaped tip. (12) Two pairs of pliers, one regular and one needle-nosed, are essential. (13) A wire cutter is built into many needle-nosed pliers. (14) A screw starter, a tool that looks like a screwdriver with a point threaded like a screw, helps to start holes in hard surfaces.

(15) Get an adjustable wrench, called a crescent wrench. (16) I'm not sure why it's called a crescent wrench. (17) Choose a mid-size wrench that adjusts to about an inch wide. (18) This size will help with various nuts and bolts. (19) A small tape measure will be useful, as will a little level, often called a torpedo level. (20) Hanging a picture is a lot easier if you can tell whether it's straight.

(21) A small saw called a keyhole saw can come in handy. (22) Be sure the one you get fits in your box. (23) Get an assortment of small nails, screws, nuts and bolts. (24) These are often packaged together. (25) A roll of picture-hanging wire and a roll of electrical tape are useful for lots of things. (26) Finally, a small flashlight is a good idea.

(27) Keep your household toolkit in a place where you can easily find it when you need it. (28) Also, always return your tools to the toolkit so that they are there when you need them.

1. Which revision would most improve the effectiveness of the first paragraph (sentences 1–4)?

   (1) remove sentence 1
   (2) remove sentence 2
   (3) remove sentence 3
   (4) remove sentence 4
   (5) no revision is necessary

2. Which revision would most improve the effectiveness of the third paragraph (sentences 7–14)?

   (1) remove sentence 8
   (2) remove sentence 10
   (3) remove sentence 12
   (4) remove sentence 13
   (5) no revision is necessary

3. Which revision would most improve the effectiveness of the fourth paragraph (sentences 15–20)?

   (1) remove sentence 15
   (2) remove sentence 16
   (3) remove sentence 17
   (4) remove sentence 19
   (5) no revision is necessary

4. Which revision would most improve the effectiveness of the fifth paragraph (sentences 21–26)?

   (1) remove sentence 21
   (2) remove sentence 22
   (3) remove sentence 23
   (4) remove sentence 24
   (5) no revision is necessary

Questions 5 through 8 refer to the following paragraph.

(1) If you could do one thing for just a few minutes a day to double or triple your child's chances for success, would you do it? (2) Well you can, and it's easier than you might imagine. (3) Imagination is so important in a child. (4) It's simple and fun, and you already know how to do it. (5) Read aloud to your child every day. (6) The difference it can make is amazing.

(7) Studies show that children whose parents read aloud to them from an early age arrive at school already equipped to do well. (8) The advantage gained will last all through school and endure through life. (9) Reading aloud with young children develops their abilities when they are most ready to learn. (10) The time spent in this way also increases their closeness to you, and it teaches them what you value because you share it with them.

(11) It is never too early to start. (12) Your child does not yet need to know how to read. (13) Even looking through picture books that have no words with your infant or toddler will produce results. (14) You can just talk about the pictures. (15) The child learns that sitting with you and a book is a time of fun and closeness. (16) It will become a time of pleasure and closeness for you as well.

(17) Set aside just a few minutes a day. (18) Bedtime is often a perfect time. (19) Pick books that are simple and fun. (20) The stories do not have to be long. (21) Ask questions about the pictures or story as you read. (22) Some of the artwork in children's books is stunningly good. (23) If your child is old enough, allow her to choose the books. (24) She may want the same one again and again, but that is perfectly all right.

(25) Reading to your children can be the most rewarding thing you ever do for them. (26) I believe this with all my heart. (27) It will also be one of the most rewarding things you do for yourself. (28) The effect lasts lifetimes—theirs and yours.

5. Which revision would improve the effectiveness of the first paragraph (sentences 1–6)?

(1) remove sentence 2
(2) remove sentence 3
(3) remove sentence 4
(4) remove sentence 6
(5) no revision is necessary

6. Which revision would improve the effectiveness of the second paragraph (sentences 7–10)?

(1) remove sentence 7
(2) remove sentence 8
(3) remove sentence 9
(4) remove sentence 10
(5) no revision is necessary

7. Which revision would improve the effectiveness of the fourth paragraph (sentences 17–24)?

(1) remove sentence 18
(2) remove sentence 19
(3) remove sentence 22
(4) remove sentence 24
(5) no revision is necessary

8. Which revision would improve the effectiveness of the final paragraph (sentences 25–28)?

(1) remove sentence 25
(2) remove sentence 26
(3) remove sentence 27
(4) remove sentence 28
(5) no revision is necessary

> **TIP**
>
> One way to check for irrelevant sentences is to determine the main idea or topic of the paragraph. If a sentence does not directly relate to this topic, the sentence may be irrelevant.

Answers and explanations start on page 120.

KEY Skill 19

Text Divisions Within Paragraphs

One writing error that you may see on the GED Writing Test is paragraphs that are too long or that contain more than one topic sentence. Paragraphs are the building blocks of a document. Each paragraph should include one main idea, stated in a topic sentence, and one or more sentences that provide supporting details.

To help readers understand information, build paragraphs that are three to six sentences long. Use these steps to make sure that paragraphs are not too long:

- Scan the document for paragraphs that have more than six sentences. Consider carefully whether these paragraphs should be divided into two.
- Look for paragraphs that discuss more than one subject or that have more than one topic sentence. Divide paragraphs as appropriate.
- Be sure that each paragraph is logically organized. Sometimes, rearranging sentences in a paragraph helps make the paragraph clearer.

Read the paragraph below. Choose the <u>one best answer</u> to the question.

(1) The notion of comfort food still exists, even in this era of fast food, take-out, and convenience foods. (2) Consider the humble grilled cheese sandwich. (3) In all these years, no one has changed or improved this sandwich. (4) Notice also that the fast-food, take-out, and convenience-food industries do not provide grilled cheese sandwiches. (5) They know that they cannot improve upon a grilled cheese sandwich from home in either price or taste. (6) Macaroni and cheese is a food that has followed a different course. (7) The convenience-food industry provides a cheap substitute far from the taste and texture of the original. (8) Is macaroni and cheese from the microwave really comfort food? (9) Millions of people eat it, perhaps because they have never had the homemade kind. (10) Hot, thick macaroni and real cheese straight from your oven brings aroma and comfort beyond anything you'll ever find in a little box.

QUESTION: Which revision would improve the effectiveness of this paragraph?

Begin a new paragraph with

    (1) sentence 4.
    (2) sentence 5.
    (3) sentence 6.
    (4) sentence 8.
    (5) no revision is necessary

EXPLANATIONS

    (1) No. Sentence 4 supports the idea in sentence 1, the topic sentence, and should not begin a new paragraph.
    (2) No. Sentence 5 also supports the idea in the topic sentence and should not begin a new paragraph.
    (3) **Yes. Sentence 6 introduces a new set of ideas, shifting to a discussion of macaroni and cheese, and should therefore begin a new paragraph.**
    (4) No. Sentence 8 supports the idea stated in sentence 6 and should not be separated from it.
    (5) No. The paragraph contains two topic sentences and should be split into two paragraphs.

ANSWER: (3) sentence 6.

Practice the Skill

Try these sample questions. Choose the <u>one best answer</u> to each question. Then check your answers and read the explanations.

(A)

(1) Sunscreen is a gel or lotion that is applied to the skin. (2) Its purpose is to block the sun's rays, thereby preventing damage to the skin. (3) Everyone should wear sunscreen, even people who don't burn. (4) Anyone planning to be in the sun for more than 20 minutes should apply sunscreen. (5) Sunlight has two types of dangerous rays. (6) Ultraviolet A (UVA) rays are known as "aging" rays; ultraviolet B (UVB) rays are "burning" rays. (7) Choose a "broad spectrum" sunscreen. (8) This type of sunscreen blocks both UVA and UVB rays.

(B)

(9) Now that you know how important sunscreen is and have bought the proper type, you should know how to apply it effectively. (10) First, apply sunscreen 15 to 30 minutes before you go outside. (11) Be generous; apply more than you think you need. (12) Then reapply the sunscreen after swimming or heavy exercise, even if the product says it is waterproof. (13) Finally, apply sunscreen even on cloudy days because UVA and UVB rays both penetrate the clouds. (14) Each sunscreen product displays an SPF (sun protection factor) rating that ranges from 2 to 80.

1. Which revision would improve the effectiveness of paragraph A?

   Begin a new paragraph with

   (1) sentence 4.
   (2) sentence 5.
   (3) sentence 6.
   (4) sentence 7.
   (5) no revision is necessary

   HINT If a paragraph seems to discuss more than one subject, it may need to be divided into two paragraphs. Read carefully to see where the subject changes.

2. Which revision would improve the effectiveness of paragraph B?

   (1) remove sentence 11
   (2) move sentence 9 to follow sentence 13
   (3) move sentence 14 to the beginning of the paragraph
   (4) remove sentence 14
   (5) no revision is necessary

   HINT A paragraph that seems to discuss more than one subject may need to be divided into two. It may also simply include a misplaced sentence.

Answers and Explanations

1. (2) sentence 5.
Option (2) is correct because sentence 5 introduces a new topic and should begin a new paragraph.

Option (1) is not correct because sentence 4 supports the topic sentence, sentence 1. Options (3) and (4) are not correct because the topic change occurs in sentence 5, and sentences 6 and 7 both support sentence 5. Option (5) is not correct because the original paragraph discusses two topics and should be divided.

2. (4) remove sentence 14
Option (4) is correct because sentence 14 states a new idea that does not support the other sentences in the paragraph.

Option (1) is not correct because sentence 11 supports the topic sentence and should not be removed. Option (2) incorrectly rearranges the sentences, putting the topic sentence near the end of the paragraph, which does not make sense. Option (3) suggests introducing the paragraph with a sentence that does not relate. Option (5) includes a sentence that does not belong in the paragraph.

Text Divisions Within Paragraphs

Directions: Choose the <u>one best answer</u> to each question.

<u>Questions 1 through 7</u> refer to the following memorandum.

Clark Systems   Date: May 15, 2009

To: Ms. Katherine Motulo, Vice-President, Administration
From: Mr. Carlos Cisneros, Director, Human Resources Development
Subject: Spouse and Family Assistance Program

(A)

(1) In recent months, many new hires and transferred employees have expressed concern over relocation problems experienced by their families. (2) Following our discussion last month, I scheduled a meeting of the Human Resources Committee. (3) Prior to the meeting, committee staff interviewed 30 new employees and their spouses. (4) This memo reports on the committee meeting and proposes a way to address the complications of relocation. (5) The current expansion of our company hinges on the continued success of our product line. (6) Providing technical services is our core business. (7) Without qualified technical personnel and support staff, our expansion cannot succeed. (8) If we cannot provide adequate relocation assistance, we will be unable to continue drawing adequate staff to Chicago. (9) Here is background information.

(B)

(10) In response to the FlightCheck contract, Clark Systems transferred several technical specialists to our headquarters. (11) Many of these transferred professionals have spouses who left their jobs to move to Chicago. (12) The financial security of many of these couples is dependent upon the spouse's finding suitable employment. (13) However, many find the Chicago job market difficult. (14) Problems in finding suitable jobs in reasonable locations contribute to the difficulties of these new residents. (15) Most of these specialists have been with Clark Systems for at least five years. (16) We have also hired many new support staff. (17) Most of these workers have young children and must arrange for child care. (18) Finding child care is a serious concern for these employees. (19) Location, cost, and quality of care are issues that contribute directly to their view of their jobs at Clark. (20) Many have expressed a desire for on-site child care.

(C)

(21) The Human Resources Committee proposes the initiation of a Spouse and Family Assistance Program. (22) A Human Resource specialist will be designated to coordinate the program. (23) This program is designed to help spouses continue their careers and to help families find housing and quality schools. (24) The program will focus on three areas: housing referral for transferred employees, employment counseling for spouses, and child-care through local agencies. (25) The HRD staff has researched the resources and costs involved. (26) These factors and many others are thoroughly covered in the attached proposal. (27) I am eager to hear your response, Katherine. (28) I'm available to answer questions and to discuss the contents of this report at any time. (29) These problems must be solved for our company.

1. Which revision would improve the effectiveness of paragraph A?

   Begin a new paragraph with

   (1) sentence 4.
   (2) sentence 5.
   (3) sentence 7.
   (4) sentence 8.
   (5) no revision is necessary

2. Which revision of sentence 9 would improve the effectiveness of the memorandum?

   (1) delete the sentence
   (2) move the sentence to the beginning of paragraph A
   (3) move the sentence to the beginning of paragraph B
   (4) move the sentence to the end of paragraph B
   (5) no revision is necessary

3. Which revision should be made to the placement of sentence 15?

   (1) move the sentence to follow sentence 10
   (2) move the sentence to follow sentence 11
   (3) move the sentence to follow sentence 12
   (4) move the sentence to follow sentence 19
   (5) no revision is necessary

4. Which revision would improve the effectiveness of paragraph B?

   Begin a new paragraph with

   (1) sentence 13.
   (2) sentence 14.
   (3) sentence 15.
   (4) sentence 16.
   (5) no revision is necessary

5. Which revision should be made to the placement of sentence 22?

   (1) move the sentence before sentence 21
   (2) move the sentence to follow sentence 24
   (3) move the sentence to follow sentence 25
   (4) move the sentence to follow sentence 26
   (5) no revision is necessary

6. Which revision would improve the effectiveness of paragraph C?

   Begin a new paragraph with

   (1) sentence 24.
   (2) sentence 25.
   (3) sentence 26.
   (4) sentence 27.
   (5) no revision is necessary

7. Which revision of sentence 29 would improve the effectiveness of the memorandum?

   (1) delete the sentence
   (2) move the sentence to the end of paragraph A
   (3) move the sentence to the end of paragraph B
   (4) move the sentence to the end of paragraph C
   (5) no revision is necessary

> **TIP**
>
> If a paragraph includes more than six sentences, consider whether it should be divided into two paragraphs. Read the sentences to decide if they are all related to the same topic, two different topics, or if one just doesn't fit with the rest.

Answers and explanations start on page 121.

Text Divisions Within Documents

One writing error that you may see on the GED Writing Test is paragraphs that are short and undeveloped. They may lack a topic sentence or enough supporting detail or seem choppy and unconnected. Remember that each **paragraph** must contain a **topic sentence** and **supporting details** to be meaningful.

A document with short, choppy paragraphs may be revised in one of three ways:

- Look for a clear topic sentence in each paragraph. Providing a topic sentence may help organize the paragraph in a meaningful way.
- Look for misplaced sentences. Does each sentence belong in the paragraph in which it is placed? Do the sentences relate to the content of another paragraph? If sentences don't belong, combine or reorganize the paragraphs.
- Look for very short paragraphs that are only one, two, or three sentences long. A short paragraph may be adequately developed, but read carefully to make sure. If the sentences do not make a completely developed paragraph, either combine them with another paragraph or develop the paragraph with more supporting details. Make sure the topic sentence relates to all the details.

Read the paragraphs below. Choose the <u>one best answer</u> to the question.

(A)

(1) Annual plants bloom and then die within one growing season. (2) Fortunately, some plants are more permanent. (3) They are called perennials, and they may live for decades.

(B)

(4) Most of these plants benefit from being divided after they spend three or more years in one place. (5) Some need to be divided every year. (6) If your plants are producing fewer blooms than usual, it is time to divide them.

QUESTION: Which revision would improve the effectiveness of the paragraphs?

(1) remove sentence 1
(2) add a topic sentence to paragraph A
(3) move sentence 4 to follow sentence 6
(4) combine paragraphs A and B
(5) no revision is necessary

EXPLANATIONS

(1) No. Sentence 1 provides important information and is supported by sentence 2, so it should not be removed.
(2) No. Though it is short, paragraph A does not need a topic sentence.
(3) No. The sequence of ideas from sentence to sentence in paragraph B makes sense as is; moving sentence 4 to follow sentence 6 would disrupt this flow.
(4) **Yes. Both paragraphs are short, and the ideas flow in a way that makes sense. These paragraphs should be combined.**
(5) No. This option is not the best answer because the content of the sentences in both paragraphs is related and the paragraphs are better combined.

ANSWER: (4) combine paragraphs A and B

Practice the Skill

Try these sample questions. Choose the <u>one best answer</u> to each question. Then check your answers and read the explanations.

(A)

(1) The process of dividing plants involves digging them up, separating them into sections, and replanting the "new" plants. (2) The task of dividing plants may occur in the spring when new growth is beginning. (3) Gardeners may also divide plants in the fall, as plants begin to go dormant.

(B)

(4) Regardless of the season, experienced gardeners work on cool, overcast days to protect exposed root systems from hot sun and drying wind. (5) They also have a bucket of fresh water on hand to keep unearthed plants moist between removal and planting.

(C)

(6) Dig deeply under the plant to remove the entire plant and its root system. (7) Discard any roots that are soft or rotten looking. (8) Pull or cut apart the roots of the plant into as many pieces as you desire.

1. Which revision would improve the effectiveness of paragraphs A and B?

   (1) combine paragraphs A and B
   (2) add a topic sentence to paragraph A
   (3) add a topic sentence to paragraph B
   (4) remove sentence 1
   (5) no revision is necessary

   HINT Look carefully at the content of sentences in short paragraphs. Are the ideas related to those in another paragraph? Should the paragraphs be combined?

2. Which topic sentence would be most effective if inserted at the beginning of paragraph C?

   (1) Make sure you have the right hand tools.
   (2) Dividing plants is actually fun, once you get used to it.
   (3) Most gardeners find that dividing plants is well worth the effort.
   (4) Follow this simple three-step procedure for dividing a plant.
   (5) no topic sentence is needed

   HINT Read a very short paragraph carefully. Is it short because it is missing something? Check to be sure that ideas are well developed.

Answers and Explanations

1. (1) combine paragraphs A and B
Option (1) is correct because the ideas in the two paragraphs are related and flow together.

Option (2) is incorrect because paragraph A already has a topic sentence. Option (3) is not correct because the ideas in sentences 4 and 5 already flow smoothly. Option (4) is not correct because sentence 1 is the topic sentence. Option (5) is not the best answer because the content of the paragraphs is related and the paragraphs are better when combined.

2. (4) Follow this simple three-step procedure for dividing a plant.
Option (4) is the best topic sentence because it states specifically what readers will learn from the paragraph.

Option (1) cannot be the topic sentence because it does not relate to the topic of the paragraph. Options (2) and (3) are not correct because they do not hint at what is to follow in the paragraph. Option (5) is not correct because the paragraph needs a topic sentence that states its main point.

Text Divisions Within Documents

Directions: Choose the **one best answer** to each question.

Questions 1 through 6 refer to the following informational document.

Dangerous Intersections and How to Stay Safe

(A)

(1) The most dangerous spots are not located in large cities. (2) Los Angeles does not have any intersections in the top ten on the list. (3) New York City doesn't either. (4) Insurance companies keep track of the most hazardous intersections in the United States, with surprising results.

(B)

(5) First, the analysis takes into account the number of accidents that are known to have occurred at a location. (6) Then the risk factor for the spot is adjusted upward for each collision that is costly in terms of property damage, physical injury, and/or loss of life. (7) In summary, an intersection makes the list if it is the scene of many serious accidents.

(C)

(8) Some intersection hazards can be fixed. (9) Two common causes of accidents include poor visibility of traffic signals and poor timing of their cycles. (10) These problems can be fixed easily by changing the length of the cycles and coordinating other signals in the area.

(D)

(11) The lights themselves can also be made larger and brighter. (12) Special left-turn lanes cut down on collisions in which a turning vehicle is broadsided by oncoming traffic. (13) Finally, the damage of rear-end collisions is minimized by using special pavement that controls skidding.

(E)

(14) Sometimes an intersection's hazards are not caused by the intersection itself but by the people who drive through it. (15) Drivers must rely on themselves rather than on the road or traffic signals to stay safe. (16) Those who observe safe driving practices will be safer than those who do not. (17) In fact, the majority of traffic accidents are caused by human error.

(F)

(18) The following driving habits will help keep you safe. (19) Don't try to beat the yellow light before it turns red. (20) Don't follow other vehicles too closely. (21) Tailgating is a frequent cause of rear-end collisions. (22) Never change lanes while you are driving through an intersection.

(G)

(23) If you are waiting at a green light to make a left turn, keep the wheels of your vehicle straight. (24) This position prevents your car from ending up in another lane if you are hit from behind. (25) Always watch for other drivers who run red lights. (26) This behavior is "don't".

(H)

(27) You can stay safe in your own town with a few simple steps. (28) Find out from the city street department or local highway department where the most hazardous intersections are. (29) Be extra alert when you drive in those areas. (30) In addition, use safe driving practices every time you drive.

1. Which revision would improve the effectiveness of paragraph A?

(1) remove sentence 1
(2) move sentence 1 to follow sentence 3
(3) remove sentence 3
(4) move sentence 4 to the beginning of the paragraph
(5) no revision is necessary

2. Which topic sentence would be most effective if inserted at the beginning of paragraph B?

(1) How do insurance companies track the age of drivers involved in accidents?
(2) Insurance companies use two indicators to identify and rate treacherous intersections.
(3) Careful evaluation of treacherous intersections occurs.
(4) Insurance companies know where the treacherous intersections are.
(5) no topic sentence is needed

3. Which revision would improve the effectiveness of paragraphs C and D?

(1) move sentence 8 to the end of paragraph C
(2) move sentence 8 to the end of paragraph D
(3) remove sentence 13
(4) combine paragraphs C and D
(5) no revision is necessary

4. Which revision should be made to the placement of sentence 17?

(1) move the sentence to the beginning of paragraph E
(2) move the sentence to follow sentence 14
(3) move the sentence to follow sentence 15
(4) move the sentence to the beginning of paragraph F
(5) no revision is necessary

5. Which revision would improve the effectiveness of paragraphs F and G?

(1) combine paragraphs F and G
(2) move sentence 18 to the beginning of paragraph G
(3) remove sentence 20
(4) remove sentence 24
(5) no revision is necessary

6. Which revision would improve the effectiveness of paragraph H?

(1) move sentence 27 to the end of the paragraph
(2) remove sentence 28
(3) move sentence 29 to follow sentence 30
(4) move sentence 29 to the beginning of the paragraph
(5) no revision is necessary

> **TIP**
>
> The presence of very short paragraphs in a piece of writing should alert you to consider whether ideas are fully developed. You might need to add sentences to complete the meaning, or you might need to combine paragraphs.

Answers and explanations start on page 122.

Test Form PA
Language Arts, Writing

Tests of
General Educational
Development

Language Arts, Writing
Official GED Practice Test

GED Testing Service
American Council on Education

LANGUAGE ARTS, WRITING, PART I

Tests of General Educational Development

Directions

The Language Arts, Writing Test measures your ability to use clear and effective written English. This test includes both multiple-choice questions and an essay. The following directions apply only to the multiple-choice section; a separate set of directions is given for the essay.

The multiple-choice section consists of passages with lettered paragraphs and numbered sentences. Some of the sentences contain an error in sentence structure, usage, or mechanics (punctuation and capitalization). After reading the numbered sentences, answer the multiple-choice questions that follow. Some questions refer to sentences that are correct as written. The best answer for these questions is the one that leaves the sentence as originally written. The best answer for some questions is the one that produces a sentence that is consistent with the verb tense and point of view used throughout the text. A passage is often repeated in order to allow for additional questions on a second page. The repeated passage is the same as the first.

You will have 83 minutes to complete this test. Spend no more than 38 minutes on the 25 multiple-choice questions, leaving the remaining time for the essay. Work carefully, but do not spend too much time on any one question. Answer every question. You will not be penalized for incorrect answers. You may begin working on the essay section of this test as soon as you complete the multiple-choice section.

Do not mark in this test booklet. Record your answers on the separate answer sheet provided. Be sure that all requested information is properly recorded on the answer sheet.

To record your answers, fill in the numbered circle on the answer sheet that corresponds to the answer you select for each question in the test booklet.

EXAMPLE:

Sentence 1: **We were all honored to meet governor Phillips and his staff.**

Which correction should be made to sentence 1?

(1) change <u>were</u> to <u>was</u>
(2) insert a comma after <u>honored</u>
(3) change <u>governor</u> to <u>Governor</u>
(4) insert a comma after <u>Phillips</u>
(5) no correction is necessary

(On Answer Sheet)

In this example, the word "governor" should be capitalized; therefore, answer space 3 would be marked on the answer sheet.

Do not rest the point of your pencil on the answer sheet while you are considering your answer. Make no stray or unnecessary marks. If you change an answer, erase your first mark completely. Mark only one answer space for each question; multiple answers will be scored as incorrect. Do not fold or crease your answer sheet. All test materials must be returned to the test administrator.

DO NOT BEGIN TAKING THIS TEST UNTIL TOLD TO DO SO

Component: 9993949140
Kit: **ISBN 0-7398-5433-X**

4   **Writing, Part I**

Directions: Choose the <u>one best answer</u> to each question.

<u>Questions 1 through 10</u> refer to the following letter of complaint.

Michael Carper, Manager
Brighton Antiques and Collectibles
1540 Park Avenue
Sweetwater, VA 23690

Dear Mr. Carper:

(A)
(1) I am now writing to complain about the poor delivery service offered by your store, as you have not replied to my repeated phone messages. (2) Not only have your delivery department wasted my time, but also it has damaged my property.

(B)
(3) When I bought a sofa from you a month ago, I was being told that it would be delivered the next day, Tuesday. (4) I waited at home all day for the delivery, but nobody came. (5) Whenever I tried calling you, your phone was busy. (6) On Wednesday mourning, you phoned to say that because the delivery truck had to have its brakes repaired, the sofa could not be delivered until the following week.

(C)
(7) That Friday the sofa arrived. (8) I was leaving for work. (9) The delivery men arrived not only at an inconvenient time, but also delivered the wrong sofa. (10) After I complained for over an hour, the delivery men returned the sofa to the store. (11) Two weeks later, they returned with the sofa I had ordered. (12) Unfortunately, as they carried it into the living room, they chipped the paint on the walls broke a vase, and scratched a chest of drawers. (13) Instead of apologizing, it was told to me it was not their responsibility.

(D)
(14) I am enclosing an estimate of $500 for the damage. (15) If you do not pay it, I will contact a lawyer.

Sincerely,
Debra Weddington
Debra Weddington

GO ON TO THE NEXT PAGE

1. Sentence 1: **I am now writing to complain about the poor delivery service offered by your store, as you have not replied to my repeated phone messages.**

    The most effective revision of sentence 1 would begin with which group of words?

    (1) Because you have not replied to my repeated phone messages, I am writing
    (2) Having written to complain, the poor delivery service
    (3) Your store, delivering poor service, and I am now phoning
    (4) I had written and am now phoning and will complain
    (5) Having delivered your store such poor service, I am now writing

2. Sentence 2: **Not only have your delivery department wasted my time, but also it has damaged my property.**

    Which correction should be made to sentence 2?

    (1) change <u>only have</u> to <u>only has</u>
    (2) remove the comma after <u>time</u>
    (3) insert <u>additionally</u> after <u>also</u>
    (4) change <u>it has</u> to <u>it have</u>
    (5) replace <u>it has</u> with <u>they have</u>

3. Sentence 3: **When I bought a sofa from you a month ago, I <u>was being told</u> that it would be delivered the next day, Tuesday.**

    Which is the best way to write the underlined portion of this sentence? If the original is the best way, choose option (1).

    (1) was being told
    (2) was told
    (3) had told
    (4) have been told
    (5) having been told

4. Sentence 5: **Whenever I tried calling <u>you, your phone was</u> busy.**

    Which is the best way to write the underlined portion of this sentence? If the original is the best way, choose option (1).

    (1) you, your phone was
    (2) you, your phone being
    (3) you, your phone is
    (4) you, and your phone was
    (5) you and your phone were

5. Sentence 6: **On Wednesday mourning, you phoned to say that because the delivery truck had to have its brakes repaired, the sofa could not be delivered until the following week.**

    Which correction should be made to sentence 6?

    (1) replace <u>mourning</u> with <u>morning</u>
    (2) insert a comma after <u>phoned</u>
    (3) insert a comma after <u>that</u>
    (4) replace <u>brakes</u> with <u>breaks</u>
    (5) remove the comma after <u>repaired</u>

6. Sentences 7 and 8: **That Friday the sofa arrived. I was leaving for work.**

    Which is the most effective combination of sentences 7 and 8?

    (1) That Friday the sofa arrived, I was leaving for work.
    (2) Leaving for work that Friday, the sofa arrived.
    (3) That Friday, as I was leaving for work, the sofa arrived.
    (4) The sofa arriving on that Friday while I was leaving for work.
    (5) That Friday, the sofa arrived and I was leaving for work.

GO ON TO THE NEXT PAGE

6   **Writing, Part I**

The letter has been repeated for your use in answering the remaining questions.

Michael Carper, Manager
Brighton Antiques and Collectibles
1540 Park Avenue
Sweetwater, VA 23690

Dear Mr. Carper:

(A)
(1) I am now writing to complain about the poor delivery service offered by your store, as you have not replied to my repeated phone messages.
(2) Not only have your delivery department wasted my time, but also it has damaged my property.

(B)
(3) When I bought a sofa from you a month ago, I was being told that it would be delivered the next day, Tuesday. (4) I waited at home all day for the delivery, but nobody came. (5) Whenever I tried calling you, your phone was busy. (6) On Wednesday mourning, you phoned to say that because the delivery truck had to have its brakes repaired, the sofa could not be delivered until the following week.

(C)
(7) That Friday the sofa arrived. (8) I was leaving for work. (9) The delivery men arrived not only at an inconvenient time, but also delivered the wrong sofa. (10) After I complained for over an hour, the delivery men returned the sofa to the store. (11) Two weeks later, they returned with the sofa I had ordered. (12) Unfortunately, as they carried it into the living room, they chipped the paint on the walls broke a vase, and scratched a chest of drawers. (13) Instead of apologizing, it was told to me it was not their responsibility.

(D)
(14) I am enclosing an estimate of $500 for the damage. (15) If you do not pay it, I will contact a lawyer.

Sincerely,
Debra Weddington
Debra Weddington

GO ON TO THE NEXT PAGE

7. Sentence 9: **The delivery men <u>arrived not only</u> at an inconvenient time, but also delivered the wrong sofa.**

Which is the best way to write the underlined portion of this sentence? If the original is the best way, choose option (1).

(1) arrived not only
(2) not only arriving
(3) arrived
(4) not only arrived
(5) only arrived

8. Sentence 11: **Two weeks later, they returned with the sofa I had ordered.**

Which revision should be made to the placement of sentence 11?

(1) remove sentence 11
(2) move sentence 11 to follow sentence 12
(3) begin a new paragraph with sentence 11
(4) move sentence 11 to the end of paragraph C
(5) move sentence 11 to the end of paragraph D

9. Sentence 12: **Unfortunately, as they carried it into the living room, they chipped the <u>paint on the walls broke</u> a vase, and scratched a chest of drawers.**

Which is the best way to write the underlined portion of this sentence? If the original is the best way, choose option (1).

(1) paint on the walls broke
(2) paint on the walls, broke
(3) paint on the walls, and broke
(4) paint, on the walls, broke
(5) paint, on the walls broke

10. Sentence 13: **Instead of apologizing, it was told to me it was not their responsibility.**

Which correction should be made to sentence 13?

(1) replace <u>apologizing</u> with <u>being apologetic</u>
(2) remove the comma after <u>apologizing</u>
(3) replace <u>it was told to me</u> with <u>they told me</u>
(4) replace <u>it was not their responsibility</u>. with <u>their responsibility it was not</u>.
(5) no correction is necessary

GO ON TO THE NEXT PAGE

8   **Writing, Part I**

<u>Questions 11 through 18</u> refer to the following recruitment letter.

Trotter Institute of
Electronics

"Training for the Future"

Mr. Carlos Montanez
286 Greencrest Street
Houston, TX 77001

Dear Mr. Montanez:

(A)
(1) What does it take to get a good job? (2) You probably have read newspaper articles about how job opportunities are declining today. (3) At the same time, however there are occupations in which opportunities are expanding. (4) The U.S. Bureau of Labor Statistics gave the following report. (5) The report states that in the next 10 years the demand for electronics technicians will increase by 21 percent. (6) As an electronics technician, you can expect to have your choice of many high-paying jobs with excellent working conditions. (7) That means that for every 10 electronics technicians now working, two more will be needed.

(B)
(8) One of the best aspects of an electronics education was that you don't ever have to leave home to get one. (9) The Trotter Institute of Electronics, offers a one-year correspondence course that leads straight to a Certificate of Electronics. (10) You could soon be on your way to a career in electronics. (11) A career filled with excitement and promise.

(C)
(12) You probably think that any course offered by the Trotter Institute would be expensive. (13) Because you get textbooks, assignments, and consultation for only $450.00, and this includes employment counseling after you graduate, this will surprise you. (14) You can see now that getting a better job is easier than you thought.

(D)
(15) To prepare for a better job with a great future, complete the enclosed registration form. (16) Within 10 days, you'll move toward an interesting and rewarding new career. (17) As mentioned above in the next 10 years the demand for electronics technicians will increase by dramatic proportions. (18) Don't wait to take advantage of this exciting career opportunity.

Yours truly,
Michael T. Langford
Michael T. Langford
Admissions Counselor

GO ON TO THE NEXT PAGE

11. Sentence 3: **At the same time, however there are occupations in which opportunities are expanding.**

    Which correction should be made to sentence 3?

    (1) insert a comma after <u>however</u>
    (2) replace <u>there</u> with <u>they're</u>
    (3) insert a comma after <u>occupations</u>
    (4) remove <u>in</u> after <u>occupations</u>
    (5) no correction is necessary

12. Sentences 4 and 5: **The U.S. Bureau of Labor <u>Statistics gave the following report</u>. <u>The report states</u> that in the next 10 years the demand for electronics technicians will increase by 21 percent.**

    Which is the best way to write the underlined portion of these sentences? If the original is the best way, choose option (1).

    (1) Statistics gave the following report. The report states
    (2) Statistics gave the following report, the report states
    (3) Statistics reporting
    (4) Statistics having reported in the
    (5) Statistics reports

13. Sentence 7: **That means that for every 10 electronics technicians now working, two more will be needed.**

    Which revision should be made to the placement of sentence 7?

    (1) move sentence 7 to follow sentence 1
    (2) move sentence 7 to follow sentence 2
    (3) move sentence 7 to follow sentence 3
    (4) move sentence 7 to follow sentence 5
    (5) move sentence 7 to the end of paragraph B

14. Sentence 8: **One of the best aspects of an electronics education was that you don't ever have to leave home to get one.**

    Which correction should be made to sentence 8?

    (1) replace <u>was</u> with <u>should be</u>
    (2) change <u>was</u> to <u>is</u>
    (3) replace <u>was</u> with <u>being</u>
    (4) replace <u>ever</u> with <u>never</u>
    (5) change <u>to leave</u> to <u>to have left</u>

15. Sentence 9: **The Trotter Institute of Electronics, offers a one-year correspondence course that leads straight to a Certificate of Electronics.**

    Which correction should be made to sentence 9?

    (1) remove the comma after <u>Electronics</u>
    (2) change <u>offers</u> to <u>offering</u>
    (3) insert a comma after <u>course</u>
    (4) change <u>leads</u> to <u>led</u>
    (5) replace <u>straight</u> with <u>strait</u>

16. Sentences 10 and 11: **You could soon be on your way to a career <u>in electronics</u>. <u>A career filled</u> with excitement and promise.**

    Which is the best way to write the underlined portion of these sentences? If the original is the best way, choose option (1).

    (1) in electronics. A career filled
    (2) in electronics, but a career filled
    (3) in electronics and in addition, the career will be filled
    (4) in electronics, a career filled
    (5) no correction is necessary

GO ON TO THE NEXT PAGE

The letter has been repeated for your use in answering the remaining questions.

Trotter Institute of
Electronics

"Training for the Future"

Mr. Carlos Montanez
286 Greencrest Street
Houston, TX 77001

Dear Mr. Montanez:

(A)
(1) What does it take to get a good job? (2) You probably have read newspaper articles about how job opportunities are declining today. (3) At the same time, however there are occupations in which opportunities are expanding. (4) The U.S. Bureau of Labor Statistics gave the following report. (5) The report states that in the next 10 years the demand for electronics technicians will increase by 21 percent. (6) As an electronics technician, you can expect to have your choice of many high-paying jobs with excellent working conditions. (7) That means that for every 10 electronics technicians now working, two more will be needed.

(B)
(8) One of the best aspects of an electronics education was that you don't ever have to leave home to get one. (9) The Trotter Institute of Electronics, offers a one-year correspondence course that leads straight to a Certificate of Electronics. (10) You could soon be on your way to a career in electronics. (11) A career filled with excitement and promise.

(C)
(12) You probably think that any course offered by the Trotter Institute would be expensive. (13) Because you get textbooks, assignments, and consultation for only $450.00, and this includes employment counseling after you graduate, this will surprise you. (14) You can see now that getting a better job is easier than you thought.

(D)
(15) To prepare for a better job with a great future, complete the enclosed registration form. (16) Within 10 days, you'll move toward an interesting and rewarding new career. (17) As mentioned above in the next 10 years the demand for electronics technicians will increase by dramatic proportions. (18) Don't wait to take advantage of this exciting career opportunity.

Yours truly,
Michael T. Langford
Michael T. Langford
Admissions Counselor

GO ON TO THE NEXT PAGE

17. Sentence 13: **Because you get textbooks, assignments, and consultation for only $450.00, and this includes employment counseling after you graduate, this will surprise you.**

The most effective revision of sentence 13 would begin with which group of words?

(1) You're in for a surprise and because you get
(2) Surprise with your textbook
(3) Because you are getting many things that will surprise you
(4) As a result of the surprise and $450.00, you get
(5) You're in for a surprise! You get

18. Sentence 17: **As mentioned above in the next 10 years the demand for electronics technicians will increase by dramatic proportions.**

Which correction should be made to sentence 17?

(1) replace <u>As mentioned</u> with <u>By mentioning</u>
(2) insert a comma after <u>above</u>
(3) change <u>will increase</u> to <u>increasing</u>
(4) insert a comma after <u>increase</u>
(5) no correction is necessary

GO ON TO THE NEXT PAGE

12   **Writing, Part I**

<u>Questions 19 through 25</u> refer to the following consumer advice.

How To Take Photographs

(A)

(1) Almost everyone have had the desire to take a picture at one time or another. (2) Some even regard photographs as an art form, while others snap pictures to send to family members. (3) Knowing some of the basics of photography will help you take better pictures.

(B)

(4) One of the first decisions to make is whether to photograph in color or you can use black and white. (5) Black-and-white photographs, still high in popularity, creates a very artistic mood. (6) Color, on the other hand, may be more appropriate for pictures of the family reunion or autumn landscapes.

(C)

(7) Film speed is also important. (8) If you are photographing in bright sunlight, you should select a film with a low speed. (9) This choice will have ensured the best possible print. (10) In low-light situations or if you are photographing rapid movement, a high-speed film is more appropriate. (11) This is because the film requires less light so you can set the shutter speed at a much faster rate to capture the action.

(D)

(12) If your camera has adjustable aperture and shutter speed settings, learning to use them can greatly enhance the quality of you're photographs. (13) Aperture refers to how wide open the lens is, which in turn determines how much light is allowed in. (14) Shutter speed describes how quickly the lens opens and shuts, controlling the amount of light that reaches the film. (15) A knowledge of these and other aspects of photography will help you to create the kinds of photos you want. (16) It takes practice, of course. (17) Practice helps you produce beautiful, memorable, and meaningful pictures.

GO ON TO THE NEXT PAGE

19. Sentence 1: **Almost everyone have had the desire to take a picture at one time or another.**

Which correction should be made to sentence 1?

(1) replace <u>Almost</u> with <u>Generally</u>
(2) change <u>have</u> to <u>has</u>
(3) insert a comma after <u>desire</u>
(4) replace <u>to take</u> with <u>of taking</u>
(5) no correction is necessary

20. Sentence 4: **One of the first decisions to make is whether to photograph in color or you can use black and white.**

Which correction should be made to sentence 4?

(1) replace <u>to make</u> with <u>one makes</u>
(2) insert <u>to</u> after <u>is</u>
(3) change <u>to photograph</u> to <u>photographing</u>
(4) replace <u>or</u> with <u>but</u>
(5) remove <u>you can use</u>

21. Sentence 5: **Black-and-white photographs, still high in <u>popularity, creates</u> a very artistic mood.**

Which is the best way to write the underlined portion of this sentence? If the original is the best way, choose option (1).

(1) popularity, creates
(2) popularity, creating
(3) popularity by creating
(4) popularity, create
(5) popularity and creating

22. Sentence 9: **This choice <u>will have ensured</u> the best possible print.**

Which is the best way to write the underlined portion of this sentence? If the original is the best way, choose option (1).

(1) will have ensured
(2) has ensured
(3) has been ensuring
(4) will ensure
(5) had ensured

23. Sentence 12: **If your camera has adjustable aperture and shutter speed settings, learning to use them can greatly enhance the quality of you're photographs.**

Which correction should be made to sentence 12?

(1) change <u>has</u> to <u>does have</u>
(2) remove the comma after <u>settings</u>
(3) change <u>learning</u> to <u>to learn</u>
(4) insert a comma after <u>them</u>
(5) replace <u>you're</u> with <u>your</u>

24. Sentences 16 and 17: **It takes practice, of course. Practice helps you produce beautiful, memorable, and meaningful pictures.**

The most effective combination of sentences 16 and 17 would include which group of words?

(1) of course, practice, helps
(2) takes practice, of course, with the help of
(3) takes practice, of course, to help you
(4) practice, of course, being beautiful,
(5) of course the practice

25. Which revision would improve the effectiveness of the document?

Begin a new paragraph with

(1) sentence 3
(2) sentence 5
(3) sentence 11
(4) sentence 13
(5) sentence 15

GO ON TO: LANGUAGE ARTS, WRITING, PART II

14

LANGUAGE ARTS, WRITING, PART II

Tests of General Educational Development

Essay Directions and Topic

Look at the box on page 15. In the box are your assigned topic and the letter of that topic.

You must write on the assigned topic ONLY.

Mark the letter of your assigned topic in the appropriate space on your answer sheet booklet. Be certain that all other requested information is properly recorded in your answer sheet booklet.

You will have 45 minutes to write on your assigned essay topic. If you have time remaining in this test period after you complete your essay, you may return to the multiple-choice section. Do not return the Language Arts, Writing Test booklet until you finish both Parts I and II of the Language Arts, Writing Test.

Two evaluators will score your essay according to its overall effectiveness. Their evaluation will be based on the following features:

- Well-focused main points
- Clear organization
- Specific development of your ideas
- Control of sentence structure, punctuation, grammar, word choice, and spelling

REMEMBER, YOU MUST COMPLETE BOTH THE MULTIPLE-CHOICE QUESTIONS (PART I) AND THE ESSAY (PART II) TO RECEIVE A SCORE ON THE LANGUAGE ARTS, WRITING TEST. To avoid having to repeat both parts of the test, be sure to do the following:

- Do not leave the pages blank.
- Write legibly <u>in ink</u> so that the evaluators will be able to read your writing.
- Write on the assigned topic. If you write on a topic other than the one assigned, you will not receive a score for the Language Arts, Writing Test.
- Write your essay on the lined pages of the separate answer sheet booklet. Only the writing on these pages will be scored.

IMPORTANT:
You may return to the multiple-choice section after you complete your essay if you have time remaining in this test period. Do not return the Language Arts, Writing booklet until you finish both Parts I and II of the Language Arts, Writing Test.

GO ON TO THE NEXT PAGE

Topic A

Suppose you had the opportunity to teach something you know to someone else.

In your essay, identify what you would teach and explain how you would teach this. Use your personal observations, experience, and knowledge to support your essay.

Part II is a test to determine how well you can use written language to explain your ideas.

In preparing your essay, you should take the following steps:

- Read the **DIRECTIONS** and the **TOPIC** carefully.
- Plan your essay before you write. Use the scratch paper provided to make any notes. These notes will be collected but not scored.
- Before you turn in your essay, reread what you have written and make any changes that will improve your essay.

Your essay should be long enough to develop the topic adequately.

END OF EXAMINATION

To determine the standard score for the *Official GED Practice Language Arts, Writing Test Form PA:*

1. Locate the number of questions the candidate answered correctly on *Part I,* the multiple-choice section of the test, in the column at the far left.
2. From that point, move horizontally across the table until you intersect the column with the candidate's estimated essay score *(Part II).* If two readers have scored the essay, an average of the two scores should be calculated. Please refer to Section II (page II-12) of the *Official GED Practice Test Administrator's Manual* for essay scoring directions.
3. The number at the intersection of the row with the appropriate multiple-choice score and the column with the appropriate estimated essay score is the *Language Arts, Writing* standard score.

Compare the candidate's standard scores to the minimum score requirements in the jurisdiction in which the GED credential is to be issued. (See *Appendix D* in the *Official GED Practice Test Administrator's Manual.*)

U.S. Edition Form PA Language Arts, Writing					
Number of Correct Answers on Part 1 (Multiple Choice)	Part II Score (Essay Score)				
	2	2.5	3	3.5	4
25	620	660	700	740	800
24	550	590	630	670	730
23	510	550	590	630	690
22	490	530	570	610	670
21	470	510	550	590	650
20	460	500	540	580	640
19	450	490	530	570	630
18	440	480	520	560	620
17	430	470	510	550	610
16	420	460	500	540	600
15	410	450	490	530	590
14	400	440	480	520	580
13	390	430	470	510	570
12	390	430	470	510	570
11	380	420	460	500	560
10	380	420	460	500	560
9	370	410	450	490	550
8	370	410	450	490	550
7	360	400	440	480	540
6	350	390	430	470	530
5	340	380	420	460	520
4	330	370	410	450	510
3	310	350	390	410	460
2	280	320	360	400	410
1	230	270	310	350	400

Note: Numbers given in the body of the table are the Language Arts, Writing weighted composite standard scores. These are estimates which approximate the GED standard score that an examinee would likely attain on the actual GED Language Arts, Writing test.

Language Arts, Writing Answers

1. 1
2. 1
3. 2
4. 1
5. 1
6. 3
7. 4
8. 3
9. 2
10. 3
11. 1
12. 5
13. 4
14. 2
15. 1
16. 4
17. 5
18. 2
19. 2
20. 5
21. 4
22. 4
23. 5
24. 3
25. 5

Pretest Answers and Explanations

1. **(4) change <u>uses</u> to <u>use</u>** Option (4) makes the verb agree in number with the plural subject *appliances*. Replacing *all* with *every*—option (1)—is incorrect and does not fix the agreement problem. Option (2) adds an unnecessary comma without fixing the agreement problem. Removing the comma after *appliances* (option 3) is incorrect because the comma is necessary to set off a prepositional phrase. Option (5) is incorrect because the singular verb *uses* does not agree in number with the plural subject *appliances*.

2. **(2) replace <u>were</u> with <u>are</u>** Option (2) corrects the verb from past to present tense, which is consistent with the tense of the paragraph. Option (1) is incorrect because it adds an unnecessary comma without fixing the tense problem. Option (3)—removing the word *conducting*—is incorrect because it doesn't fix the tense problem and removes a word that is key to the meaning of the sentence. Changing *paths* to *path's* (option 4) wrongly changes a plural noun to a single possessive noun without fixing the tense problem. Option (5) is incorrect because the past-tense verb needs to be corrected to present tense to make the sentence consistent with the rest of the paragraph.

3. **(5) are overused, the copper** Option (5) corrects the sentence fragment in sentence 6, joining a dependent and an independent clause with a comma and forming a complete sentence. Option (1), which leaves the punctuation of the sentences as is, is incorrect because sentence 6 is a fragment. Removing the period after *overused* (option 2) or replacing the period after *overused* with *so* (option 3) or *and* (option 4) are incorrect because they would form run-on sentences.

4. **(1) replace <u>It</u> with <u>This overheating</u>** Option (1) correctly supplies a noun phrase to replace the pronoun, which makes the antecedent clear. Option (2) is incorrect because replacing *It* with *That* substitutes one pronoun for another, but the antecedent is still unclear. Inserting *single* before *most* (option 3) or *these* before *household* (option 4) is incorrect because these options do not correct the missing antecedent for *It*. Option (5) is incorrect because the pronoun needs to be replaced with a noun or noun phrase to be clear.

5. **(3) change <u>are</u> to <u>is</u>** Option (3) corrects a common agreement error that occurs when the subject and the verb are separated by phrases or clauses. The verb must be singular to agree with the subject *portion*. Replacing *portion* with *part* (option 1) is incorrect because it does not fix the agreement error. Inserting a comma after *rooms* (option 2) does not fix the agreement error and adds confusing and unnecessary punctuation. Removing *of the business* (option 4) takes away a necessary part of the sentence and does not fix the agreement error. Option (5) is incorrect because the plural verb *are* does not agree in number with the singular noun phrase *portion of the business*.

6. **(2) sentence 5** The first paragraph covers two topics—the many children treated in emergency rooms and the experience of the visit—that would be better broken into two paragraphs when the focus switches from the first subject to the second topic (option 2). Beginning a new paragraph with sentence 4 (option 1) is not the best choice because sentence 4 continues the subject of children treated in emergency rooms by giving the most common reasons for such visits. Beginning new paragraphs after sentences 6 or 7 (options 3 and 4) are not

good choices because they make paragraph breaks within the group of sentences that relate to parents' and children's experiences of emergency room visits and are better left in the same paragraph. (Option 5) is incorrect because the single paragraph would be better broken into two at the point the focus switches.

7. **(1) insert a comma after <u>can</u>** Option (1) correctly separates a dependent clause from an independent clause. Option (2) is incorrect because changing *encourage* to *encourages* creates a subject-verb agreement error without addressing the problem of the clauses running together without punctuation. Options (3) and (4)—changing the possessive pronoun *their* to *they're*, a contraction of *they are*, or inserting a comma after *children*—are incorrect because they introduce new mistakes without fixing the original problem of missing punctuation between the clauses. Option (5) is incorrect because the dependent clause should be set off from the independent clause with a comma.

8. **(4) Although you are anxious, you need to focus on the child, who needs to be reassured and takes cues from parents on how to react to situations.** Option (4) effectively combines sentences and eliminates repetition. Option (1) is not the best answer because while it combines sentences, it incorrectly substitutes *which* for the noun phrase *The child* to refer to a person, and doesn't eliminate much repetition. Changing the period at the end of sentence 8 to a comma (option 2) is incorrect because it creates a comma splice of two independent sentences wrongly joined only by a comma. Option (3) is incorrect because it shuffles some words and removes others to create a sentence that is nonsensical. Option (5) is not the best choice because combining the sentences could improve them by eliminating repetition.

9. **(5) need to be patient. There is** Option (5) correctly makes two complete sentences. Option (1) is incorrect because it leaves the comma splice as is. Option (2) adds *and* after the comma to make a compound sentence, but this is not the best choice because the second clause more effectively explains the first if separated into its own sentence. Option (3) is incorrect because while removing the comma avoids the comma splice, it creates a run-on sentence. Option (4) is not the best choice because while it avoids the comma splice, the insertion of *however* does not make sense in the context of the sentence.

10. **(2) Many soldiers say that fear is paralyzing. (Sentence 17)** This sentence is irrelevant and does not relate to the topic of children in emergency rooms. It should be removed (option 2). Options (1), (3), (4), and (5) are incorrect choices because sentences 16, 18, 20, and 21 all contain important and relevant information.

11. **(3) all departments. This will happen** Option (3) is the correct choice because it creates two complete sentences. Option (1), which makes no changes to the sentence, is incorrect because the sentence is a run-on. Inserting a comma after *departments* (option 2) is incorrect because it does not fix the run-on sentence and introduces a comma splice. Inserting *when* after *departments* (option 4) does not make sense in the context of the sentence and doesn't repair the run-on. Inserting a comma and *which* after *departments* (option 5) is incorrect because *which* should be

used to introduce a restrictive clause, but here it incorrectly joins two independent clauses to create a nonsensical construction.

12. **(2) replace very with vary** Option (2) correctly replaces the wrong word with the correct homonym—one of two or more words pronounced alike but different in meaning or spelling. *Vary* means "to alter," which is the sense intended here. Option (1) is not the best choice because it unnecessarily changes the verb tense (from *will hold* to *will be holding*) and does not fix the incorrect use of the homonym *very*. Option (3) incorrectly changes the preposition *from* to *to* without addressing the homonym problem in *very*. Option (4) incorrectly changes the preposition *to* to the conjunction *and* and does not fix the homonym problem. Option (5) is incorrect because *very* is an incorrect word choice and should be replaced with its homonym *vary*.

13. **(4) running smoothly, problems will be met** Option (4) correctly changes from past to future tense to indicate an action that will come in the future, as the meaning of the sentence requires. Option (1) is incorrect because it leaves the sentence as it stands; the action indicated does not occur in the past, so the past tense *were* does not make sense. Likewise, option (2), which inserts a period after *smoothly*, is incorrect because it does not change the incorrect verb *were*. Option (3) incorrectly removes the comma after *smoothly*, creating a run-on without addressing the sequence-of-tenses problem. Option (5) is incorrect. It changes *were* to *are*, but the sense of the sentence requires the shift of verb tense to the future (*will be*), not the present.

14. **(1) change departments to department's** Option (1) correctly uses the possessive form with the required apostrophe. Option (2) incorrectly changes a possessive pronoun (*your*) to the contraction for *you are* (*you're*) and doesn't provide the missing apostrophe for *departments*. Option (3) makes an unnecessary change from *two-week* to *two-weeks* and does not correct the missing possessive on *departments*. Option (4) is incorrect because it replaces *departments*, which has a singular meaning in the sentence and needs an apostrophe before the *s*, with the plural possessive form *departments'*. Option (5) is incorrect because the singular possessive form is required for *departments*.

15. **(5) In addition, I have run programs** Option (5) correctly substitutes the transition words *In addition* for *Finally* to signal that this sentence's ideas will add to those that precede it. Option (1) is not the best choice because it makes no revision of the original sentence, in which the transition word *Finally* is confusing, when there are more ideas to come in the paragraph. Option (2) incorrectly changes the tense (*I have* to *I had*), which is confusing because the writer doesn't mean to indicate that running the program was a thing of the past, but that it is ongoing. Option (3)—omitting the transition word *Finally* and changing the word *have* to *will*—is not the best choice because including transition words would make the paragraph's ideas clearer, and the writer is explaining what he currently does, not what he will be doing in the future. Option (4) incorrectly uses *Whenever*, which does not make sense in the sentence or provide the necessary transition to clarify the paragraph's ideas.

16. **(2) replace they with them** Option (2) correctly uses the pronoun needed for the object *help*. Option (1) is incorrect because it inserts an unnecessary comma after *parents* and does not fix the pronoun problem. Option (3) is incorrect because it replaces a correct possessive pronoun with the contraction for *they are* but doesn't repair the pronoun problem. Option (4) is incorrect because it inserts an unnecessary comma after *relationships* but doesn't fix the pronoun problem. Option (5) is incorrect because the pronoun *they* is wrongly used in the sentence to refer to the object *help*.

17. **(2) The keys to the program were active listening, careful restating, and withholding judgment.** Option (2) correctly demonstrates parallel structure, in which equal and related words and phrases in a series (*a, b,* and *c*) must use the same grammatical form. Option (1) incorrectly changes the verb *were* to *was* and does not address the parallel structure problem. Option (3) wrongly inserts a comma after the verb and does not address the parallel structure problem. Option (4) is incorrect because while the series achieves parallel structure, it changes the meaning of the sentence to indicate that making judgments is a positive thing. Option (5) rephrases the series but does not achieve parallel structure in the elements' form.

18. **(3) combine (C) and (D) into a single paragraph** Option (3) correctly ends the letter with a single, fluid paragraph rather than the two short, choppy ones. Reversing the order of the last two paragraphs (option 1) does not make logical sense or improve the division of text at the end of the letter. Removing paragraphs C or D (options 2 and 4) incorrectly removes important information. Option (5) is not the best choice because it does not improve the choppiness of the final two paragraphs.

19. **(1) remove comma after find** Option (1) correctly removes an unnecessary comma. Option (2) makes a change in verb tense that is not logical (*find* to *had found*) and does not remove the unnecessary comma. Option (3) incorrectly inserts a second unnecessary comma after *vigorous* and does not remove the first one after *find*. Option (4) incorrectly changes the pronoun *them* to *themselves* and does not remove the unnecessary comma. Option (5) is incorrect because the comma after *find* is unnecessary and should be removed.

20. **(5) The key to controlling stress is to relax.** The paragraph is about the relationship between stress and relaxation. Option (5) best signals the subject of the paragraph in a clear topic sentence. Options (1) and (2) are not the best choices because while they are strong openers, they do not signal to readers that the paragraph is about relaxation. Option (3) is incorrect because it adds an irrelevant personal detail of how the writer fights stress. Option (4) is not the best choice because while it is true that stress is different for every person, this merely adds a detail about relaxation.

Answers and Explanations

Skill 1 Sentence Fragments
Pages 12–13

1. **(3) Telecommuting is working** Option (3) corrects the sentence fragment by adding the verb *is* to make sentence 2 complete. Option (1) is incorrect because the group of words is a fragment. Option (2) adds a comma, but the sentence still doesn't make sense without a verb. The words *and* (option 4) and *because* (option 5) don't correct the sentence fragment because it still lacks a verb; they just create new sentence fragments.

2. **(5) no correction is necessary** The original sentence is correct as written. The commas in options (1) and (2) should not be removed because they correctly set off the phrase *wearing whatever is comfortable,* so they are necessary. In option (3), adding the word *when* makes the sentence illogical. Option (4) turns the sentence into a comma splice.

3. **(1) reasons, such as increased** Option (1) is correct because adding a comma and the words *such as* changes the complete sentence 5 and fragment sentence 6 into a single complete sentence. Options (2) and (5) create a dependent clause that does not logically connect to sentence 5. Replacing the period between the sentences with a comma (option 3) creates a comma splice, or run-on sentence. Option (4) does not fix the fragment because a semicolon alone cannot be used to combine a fragment and an independent clause.

4. **(1) replace Because telecommuters with Telecommuters** Option (1) is correct since removing the word *Because* changes a sentence fragment into a complete sentence. Option (2) does not fix the dependent clause by replacing *Because* with *Since*. Inserting a comma after *need* (option 3) or removing *however* (option 4) does not make the dependent clause a complete sentence. Option (5) is incorrect since the word *Because* creates a dependent clause that has no related independent clause and is not a complete sentence.

5. **(2) This technology is global positioning.** Option (2) is correct because it supplies a subject and a verb to make the sentence complete. Option (1) is incorrect because the original group of words lacks a verb. Option (3) is incorrect because it does not supply a subject to complete the sentence. Option (4) includes an unnecessary comma after the word *called*, which creates a grammatically incorrect sentence. Substitution of a semicolon for the period following *positioning* (option 5) does not fix the fragment because it is still not complete.

6. **(3) very precise data to special receivers** Option (3) is correct because sentence 4 is a fragment lacking a verb. Adding *to* connects the fragment to the verb *beam,* which makes a complete sentence. Option (1) is incorrect because sentence 4 is a fragment. Option (2) deletes the word *Special* but does not change sentence 4 from a fragment. Option (4) adds the word *receiver* before *data*, which incorrectly changes the meaning of the sentences. Option (5) forms a sentence that is grammatically complete but doesn't make sense because the receivers are not being beamed to data but vice versa.

7. **(1) replace Although then with Then** Option (1) is correct because the original sentence fragment is a dependent clause and removing *Although* makes the sentence complete. Inserting a comma after *device* (option 2), changing *lets* to *let's* (option 3), or adding *at* to the end of the sentence (option 4) does not change the group of words from a fragment. Option (5) is incorrect because the original sentence is a fragment that starts with a dependent clause and needs an independent clause to complete it.

8. **(5) no correction is necessary** Option (5) is correct because the sentence is complete and clear as written. Removing the comma after *devices* (option 1) results in a sentence that is still complete but less clear. Inserting a period after *devices* and capitalizing *hikers* (option 2) results in two sentence fragments. Adding a comma after *drivers* (option 3) is unnecessary. Replacing *hikers or drivers* with *receivers* (option 4) changes the meaning of the sentence so that it no longer makes sense.

9. **(4) moving or stationary, could be** Option (4) combines the fragments in sentences 7 and 8 into a single complete sentence with a subject and a verb. The original phrasing (option 1) is incorrect because sentence 7 is a sentence fragment. Option (2) creates a run-on sentence. Option (3) misplaces the comma. Using a semicolon to replace the period following *stationary* (option 5) does not fix the fragment because a semicolon alone cannot be used to combine a fragment and an independent clause.

Skill 2 Run-On Sentences
Pages 16–17

1. **(2) back injuries, ruining** Option (2) is correct because it joins an independent clause and a dependent clause with a comma to make a complete sentence. The original sentence, option (1), is incorrect because it is a comma splice: two independent clauses joined by a comma. Options (3) and (4) incorrectly use a semicolon to join dependent and independent clauses. Option (5) subordinates the second clause to the first, which results in a sentence that doesn't make sense.

2. **(5) no correction is necessary** While the original sentence, (option 5), is a long sentence, it is clear and grammatically correct. Option (1) is incorrect because it creates a fragment in the second sentence, which lacks a subject and verb. Replacing the comma after *saying* with a semicolon (option 2) results in a sentence fragment. Inserting a comma after *choices* (option 3) is incorrect because it adds an unnecessary comma. Option (4) is incorrect because it is awkward and would require that the quotation marks be removed for the sentence to make sense.

3. **(4) Also, avoid packing a separate outfit for each day.** Option (4) correctly repairs the run-on sentence and states the idea that the original sentence implied. Option (1) does not fix the run-on sentence. Options (2) and (5) are both confusing and grammatically incorrect. Option (3) is incorrect because it changes the meaning of the original sentence.

4. **(2) tops and shirts. Then use** Option (2) is correct because it breaks the run-on sentence into two sentences. The original sentence (option 1) is incorrect because it is a run-on sentence that combines too many ideas. Option (3) is incorrect because it is a comma splice that incorrectly joins two independent clauses with a comma. Option (4) implies an unnecessary contrast of ideas and does not repair the run-on sentence. The semicolon and additional phrase (option 5)

are incorrect, because adding a semicolon after *tops* creates an independent clause, which adds even more to an already bulky sentence.

5. **(3) pronounce *scherzo*, reach** Option (3) is correct because the *if* construction subordinates the first clause, making *reach* the verb of an independent clause. The original sentence (option 1) is incorrect because it is a run-on sentence. Options (2) and (5) are incorrect because adding a period or semicolon after *scherzo* results in two sentence fragments, or dependent clauses joined by a comma. Option (4) does not repair the run-on sentence.

6. **(4) a lot of words. It is** Option (4) is correct because breaking the run-on into complete sentences, each with a subject and verb, works best. The original sentence (option 1) is incorrect because it is a run-on sentence. Deleting *it* (option 2) does not correct the run-on. Inserting a comma after *words* (option 3) is incorrect because it does not repair the run-on and results in a comma splice: two independent clauses joined by a comma. Replacing *it* with *that* (option 5) does not correct the sentence and makes it even more confusing.

7. **(5) no correction is necessary** Option (5) is correct because the original sentence is complete, including a subject and verb and correctly punctuating a series of ideas. Adding a period after *Independence* (option 1) creates a fragment. Inserting a comma after *text* (option 2) is incorrect because it adds a needless comma to a sentence that is already complete. Removing the comma after *Independence* (option 3) creates a mistake in list punctuation. Replacing *and* with *although* (option 4) subordinates the last group of words in a way that makes no sense.

8. **(2) world, although** Option (2) is correct because it deletes the repetition of conjunctions and still relates the differing ideas in the sentence. Options (1) and (3) are both incorrect because the sentence doesn't make sense with two conjunctions, *although* and *however*, being placed side by side. The shortened sentence in option (4) is not correct because it creates a run-on sentence. Option (5) is not correct because there should not be two conjunctions used side by side.

9. **(2) students, dictionaries even** Option (2) is correct because it subordinates a dependent clause (*A great reference for students*) to the independent clause that follows the comma. Option (1) is incorrect because the subject of the sentence is *dictionaries*, not *students*. Options (3) and (5) are incorrect because they are run-on sentences. Option (4) incorrectly changes the meaning of the sentence.

KEY Skill 3 Comma Splices
Pages 20–21

1. **(3) insert *but* after the comma** Adding the conjunction *but* (option 3) correctly links the clauses into a single complete sentence that makes sense. Replacing *Sailplane* with *When sailplane* (option 1) is incorrect because it subordinates the first clause in a way that doesn't make sense. Inserting the conjunction *or* after the comma (option 2) wrongly suggests an either-or construction. Option (4) is wrong because it creates a run-on sentence in which the two clauses are joined without punctuation to separate them. Option (5) is wrong because the original sentence is a comma splice and thus needs a correction.

2. **(5) no correction is necessary** The original sentence is correct as written. Changing *Using* to *Use* (option 1) is incorrect because it creates a comma splice. Option (2) is not the best option because it only adds an unnecessary comma. Inserting *and* after the comma (option 3) and removing the comma (option 4) are incorrect because both create a run-on sentence.

3. **(4) day, and they can cover** Option (4) corrects the comma splice by joining the two clauses with the coordinating conjunction *and*. Option (1) is incorrect because the sentence is a comma splice. Option (2) is incorrect because it creates a run-on sentence. While options (3) and (5) insert a coordinating conjunction, *but*, and the conjunction *when* after the comma to repair the comma splice, the word choice does not make sense in either option because *but* implies contrast and *when* implies time, neither of which are referred to in the context of the sentence.

4. **(4) noise, although he feels** Option (4) is correct because inserting *although* after the comma correctly subordinates the second clause to the first. The original (option 1) is incorrect because it is a comma splice. Option (2) is incorrect because it creates a run-on sentence. Option (3) is incorrect because replacing the comma with the conjunction *or* wrongly suggests an either-or construction. Option (5) is incorrect because replacing the comma with a period and *Though* turns the second clause into a sentence fragment, or incomplete thought.

5. **(2) freedom. They also experience** Option (2) is correct because it inserts a period to break the comma splice into two clear sentences. Option (1) is incorrect because it is a comma splice. Option (3) is incorrect because even with the addition of *however*, the sentence is still a comma splice. Removing the comma (option 4) is incorrect because it creates a run-on sentence. Replacing the comma with *whenever* (option 5) creates a run-on sentence, which would be incorrect.

6. **(3) diary; the parents** Option (3) is correct because replacing the comma with a semicolon repairs the comma splice. Option (1) is incorrect because it is a comma splice. Option (2) is incorrect because it creates a run-on sentence. Options (4) and (5) are incorrect because adding the coordinating conjunctions *but* and *or* do not make sense in the sentence.

7. **(5) no correction is necessary** The sentence is correct as written. Inserting a period after *problems* (option 1) is incorrect because it creates a fragment. Option (2) is incorrect because it adds an unnecessary comma after *problems*. Inserting *although* after *problems* (option 3) is incorrect because it does not make sense in the sentence. Option (4) incorrectly inserts a comma between the noun *problems* and its modifier (*prenatal*).

8. **(3) medications, and it should note** Option (3) is correct because inserting the conjunction *and* after the comma links the two clauses and repairs the comma splice. Option (1) is incorrect because it is a comma splice. Option (2) is incorrect because deleting the comma creates a run-on sentence. Adding *however* (option 4) creates a run-on sentence. Option (5) is illogical and creates a sentence fragment.

9. **(1) By maintaining useful records, parents can supply invaluable information to medical professionals.** Option (1) is correct because it subordinates the first clause and relates it to the second. Option (2) is incorrect because the sentence remains a comma splice, even after adding *however*. Option (3) is incorrect because it creates a fragment of the phrase after the period. Option (4) adds unnecessary words that make the sentence illogical and grammatically incorrect. The original sentence (option 5) is incorrect because it is a comma splice.

KEY Skill 4 Combining Sentences
Pages 24–25

1. **(4) water daily; therefore a family** Option (4) correctly combines the sentences with a semicolon, and *therefore* shows the relationship between the ideas. Option (1) is incorrect because it creates a comma splice. Option (2) is incorrect because the conjunctive adverb *instead* does not make sense with the sentences. Option (3) incorrectly creates a comma splice and *however* is illogical. Option (5) creates a run-on sentence.

2. **(4) enormous, but they** Option (4) adds the coordinating conjunction *but* to correctly relate the ideas and show their contrast. Option (1) is not correct because the sentences can be combined. Option (2) is incorrect because introducing the subordinate conjunction *whenever* results in a sentence that does not make sense. Option (3) is incorrect because *thus* changes the meaning of the sentences. Option (5) is incorrect because it incorrectly subordinates the second clause.

3. **(2) gallons; however, running** Option (2) correctly uses a semicolon and a comma with the conjunctive adverb *however*. The conjunctions *so* (option 1) and *for* (option 4) incorrectly imply a logical progression that changes the meaning of the sentence. Options (3) and (5) are incorrect because they change the meaning of the sentence.

4. **(4) gallon with each brushing.** Using a prepositional phrase (option 4) effectively eliminates repetition of ideas. Option (1) is ineffective because it combines the ideas without eliminating the repetition. Option (2) is incorrect because it incorrectly subordinates the second clause. Options (3) and (5) are incorrect because they merely repeat the ideas.

5. **(2) Clean water will be ever more important in the future, so we should conserve it.** Option (2) is correct because the conjunction *so* combines the ideas and shows their relationship. Option (1) is incorrect because it creates a comma splice. Option (3) is incorrect because the subordinate conjunction *although* changes the meaning of the sentence. Option (4) is incorrect because it is a run-on. Option (5) is incorrect because *next* also changes and confuses the meaning.

6. **(4) boiled; however, it shouldn't** Option (4) is correct because it uses a semicolon and the conjunctive adverb *however* to combine the ideas and show the contrast between them. Option (1) is incorrect because it creates a comma splice. In option (2), *so* incorrectly makes an illogical relationship between the two ideas, as does *because* (option 3). Option (5) is incorrect because it doesn't make sense to simply join the two sentences when their meanings contrast.

7. **(3) cooked, but it** Option (3) adds the coordinating conjunction *but* to smoothly relate the ideas and correctly show contrast. Option (1), the original sentence, is incorrect because there is an effective way to join the sentences. Option (2) is not the best choice because it does not contrast the two sentences adequately. Option (4) incorrectly uses a comma alone with the conjunctive adverb, and *moreover* doesn't make sense. Option (5) is incorrect because it creates a comma splice.

8. **(1) water, so it will** Option (1) correctly joins two ideas and shows their relationship. Option (2) is incorrect because it is a run-on that does not make sense. Option (3) is incorrect because *however* changes the meaning, as does *but* (option 5). Option (4) is incorrect because it creates a comma splice.

9. **(4) pot, and when** Option (4) joins the sentences in a logical sequence. Options (1) and (3) are incorrect because the conjunctive adverbs *therefore* and *similarly* change the meaning of the sentence. Option (2) incorrectly uses the coordinating conjunction *but*, which changes the meaning of the sentence by implying a contrasting relationship where there is none. Option (5) is incorrect because it creates a comma splice.

10. **(1) well steamed. Before you** Option (1) is correct; the sentences are correct as written. Option (2) is incorrect because it breaks the sentences in the wrong place. Option (3) is incorrect because it creates a run-on. Option (4) is incorrect because it creates a comma splice. Option (5) is incorrect because adding the conjunctive adverb *however* changes the meaning of the sentence.

Skill 5 Parallel Structure
Pages 28–29

1. **(1) remove most people think** Removing *most people think* (option 1) correctly leaves the sentence with a parallel series of adjectives: *ancient, respected, and attractive.* Option (2) is incorrect because the article *an* is required to maintain parallel structure. Options (3) and (4) are incorrect because they add the unnecessary articles *a* before *respected* and *an* before *attractive*. The original sentence (option 5) is incorrect because it is a non-parallel series.

2. **(5) long legs,** The words *long legs* (option 5) correctly provide the adjective/noun pair that is parallel to the other items in the series. Option (1) is incorrect because *having* is a verb form that alters the parallel structure. Option (2) is incorrect because *has* is also a verb form that makes the structure non-parallel. Option (3) incorrectly includes a subordinate idea (*that are long*), which is not parallel to the other items in the series. Option (4) is incorrect because *runs* introduces a verb not parallel to the other adjective/noun pairs in the series.

3. **(5) no correction is necessary** Option (5) is correct because the adjectives *thick, long,* and *flowing* are already parallel. Option (1) is incorrect because it alters the parallel structure by using the verb form *flow*. Option (2) is not the best choice because it is unnecessarily wordy and awkward. Option (3) is incorrect because commas are required in the series. Option (4) is incorrect because it includes a non-parallel verb (*has*).

4. (2) sweet Option (2) is correct because the word *sweet* is an adjective and uses the same grammatical form as *aloof* and *stubborn*, resulting in parallel structure. Options (1) and (4) incorrectly put the verbs *have* and *are* in the series of adjectives. Option (3) incorrectly includes the adverb *sweetly*. Option (5) is incorrect because *with a sweet disposition* is a prepositional phrase not parallel with the adjectives in the series.

5. (2) to be by themselves The first two items in the series are infinitive phrases, so (option 2) is parallel. Options (1), (3), (4), and (5) are incorrect because each uses a verb phrase rather than an infinitive phrase beginning with *to be*.

6. (4) falling leaves. Option (4) is correct because *falling leaves* creates an adjective/noun pair that is parallel to other items in the series. Options (1), (2), (3), and (5) are incorrect because they do not follow the adjective/noun pattern.

7. (4) change <u>yellow that shines</u> to <u>shining yellow</u> The existing items in the series are adjective/noun combinations, so *shining yellow* (option 4) is the correct choice. Options (1) and (2) incorrectly insert unneeded verbs in the series. Option (3) is wordy and does not correct the non-parallel structure. Removing *in autumn* (option 5) is incorrect as it does not fix the non-parallel structure.

8. (3) change <u>it sparkles</u> to <u>sparkling</u> Option (3) is correct because *sparkling* is an adjective, as are the first two items in the series, *blue* and *clear*. Option (1) incorrectly inserts the unneeded verb *is* in the series. Option (2) incorrectly inserts the unneeded pronoun *it* in the series. Option (4) incorrectly substitutes a relative pronoun for an article and does not correct the non-parallel structure. Option (5) is incorrect because a change is needed.

9. (2) and photographers. The series contains nouns, so (option 2) is needed to complete the parallel structure. The original sentence (option 1) is not correct because it is not parallel to the nouns in the series. Options (3) and (4) are incorrect because they lack the coordinating conjunction *and*. Option (5) is incorrect because the verb phrase is not parallel to the existing nouns in the series.

KEY **Skill 6 Verb Tenses**
Pages 32–33

1. (3) change <u>had called</u> to <u>call</u> Option (3) correctly uses a simple present-tense verb, *call*, for a condition taking place in the present. Options (1), (2), and (4) are incorrect because they suggest future-tense verbs (*will call, will have called, will be calling*) for a present condition. Option (5) incorrectly suggests a past continuous verb, *were calling*, for a present condition.

2. (2) fought Option (2) correctly uses the simple past-tense verb *fought* for action that took place in the past, as indicated by "in 490 B.C." Option (1) incorrectly uses a present continuous verb, *are fighting*, for action in the past. Option (3) incorrectly uses a simple present-tense verb, *fight*, for action in the past. Option (4) incorrectly uses a future continuous verb, *will be fighting*, for action in the past. Option (5) incorrectly uses a present perfect verb, *have fought*, for action in the past.

3. (5) no correction is necessary Option (5) is correct because the sentence is correct as written. Option (1)

incorrectly uses a present continuous verb, *are sending*, for action in the past: Option (2) incorrectly uses a future perfect verb, *will be sent*, for action in the past. Option (3) incorrectly uses a simple present-tense verb, *send*, for action in the past. Option (4) uses the past continuous verb *were sending* but is incorrect because the action in the sentence is complete and not continuous.

4. (4) delivered news of the victory; then he collapsed Option (4) correctly uses the simple past-tense verbs, *delivered* and *collapsed*, for action in the past. Option (1) incorrectly uses a simple present-tense verb, *collapses*, for action in the past. Option (2) uses a past continuous verb, *was delivering*, but the action is not continuous. Option (3) uses a future perfect verb, *will have collapsed*, for action in the past. Option (5) incorrectly uses a past perfect verb, *had delivered*, and fails to correct the incorrect *collapses*.

5. (1) change <u>were honoring</u> to <u>have honored</u> Option (1) correctly uses a present perfect-tense verb, *have honored*, for an action completed in the present. Options (2) and (3) both suggest continuous verb forms (present, *are honoring*, and future, *will be honoring*), but the action is not continuous. Option (4) incorrectly uses a simple future-tense verb, *will honor*, for an action completed in the present. Option (5) incorrectly uses a past continuous verb form, *were honoring*, for an action completed in the present.

6. (4) recently saw a terrifying accident Option (4) correctly uses the simple past-tense verb *saw* for action in the past. Option (1) uses an incorrect form, *seen*, for the simple past tense. Option (2) incorrectly uses the past perfect form *had seen* where the simple past-tense verb *saw* is better. Option (3) incorrectly uses a simple future-tense verb, *will see*, for action in the past. Option (5) incorrectly uses a present perfect verb, *was seeing*, for action in the past.

7. (1) change <u>will walk</u> to <u>walked</u> Option (1) correctly replaces the simple future-tense verb *will walk* with the simple past-tense verb *walked*. Option (2) incorrectly uses a present continuous verb, *is walking*, for an action in the past. Option (3) incorrectly uses a present perfect verb, *has walked*, for an action in the past. Option (4) incorrectly uses a simple present-tense verb, *walk*, for an action in the past. Option (5) incorrectly uses a future continuous verb, *will be walking*, for action in the past.

8. (5) change <u>hasn't thought</u> to <u>hadn't thought</u> Option (5) correctly replaces the present perfect verb *hasn't thought* with the past perfect verb *hadn't thought* to refer to an action completed in the past. Options (1) and (2) incorrectly suggest changes to the correct simple past-tense verb *saw*. Option (3) incorrectly uses a simple future-tense verb, *will think*, for an action completed in the past. Option (4) incorrectly uses a present continuous verb, *isn't thinking*, for an action completed in the past.

9. (1) change <u>said</u> to <u>says</u> Option (1) correctly uses the simple present tense for present action, as indicated by the word *Now*. Option (2) incorrectly uses a simple future-tense verb, *will say*, for present action. Option (3) incorrectly uses a past perfect verb, *had said*, for present action. Options (4) and (5) incorrectly change *will never again drive*, which needs no correction.

Skill 7 Sequence of Tenses
Pages 36–37

1. **(5) no correction is necessary** Option (5) is correct because the sentence is correct as written. Options (1) and (2) incorrectly suggest past-tense verbs (the simple past-tense verb *was* and the past continuous verb *had been*) to state a present condition, which can be seen in the rest of the paragraph. Option (3) suggests incorrectly changing the correct past-tense form to the present-tense verb *exports*. Option (4) incorrectly uses the past-tense verb *were* to state a present condition.

2. **(2) change grew to grows** Option (2) correctly uses a present-tense verb, *grows*, that is consistent with both the other verb in the sentence, *exports*, and the present tense established by other information in the paragraph. Option (1) is incorrect because it changes the past-tense verb *grew* not to the correct verb tense but to the adjective *grown*. Option (3) suggests the past-tense verb *exported*, which is consistent with the other verb in the sentence but is not consistent with the rest of the paragraph. Option (4) incorrectly suggests the future tense, *will export*. Option (5) uses a past-tense verb, *grew*, which is inconsistent with the other verb in this sentence and other information in the paragraph.

3. **(1) still produce** Option (1) is correct because the planting of the vineyards occurred in the past, while the producing occurs in the present. Option (2) unnecessarily uses the future tense (*will produce*). Option (3) incorrectly uses the past-tense verb *produced* to tell about an action in the present. Option (4) incorrectly uses the present perfect verb *have produced* for an activity that is still taking place, not completed in the present. Option (5) is incorrect because it uses the future continuous verb *will be producing*.

4. **(3) change came to come** Option (3) correctly changes the past perfect form of the verb to present perfect. Option (1) incorrectly changes the meaning of the sentence by removing the verb *came* and keeping only the helping verb *have*. Option (2) incorrectly leaves the past-tense verb *came* and changes the present-tense verb *rely* to an inflected form (*relying*). Option (4) unnecessarily uses the future tense. The original (option 5) incorrectly pairs the present-tense helping verb *have* with the past-tense verb *came*.

5. **(2) have grown** Option (2) correctly uses the present perfect verb *have grown* to describe an action completed in the present. Options (1) and (4) are incorrect because they use future-tense verbs (*will have grown* and *will grow*) to describe present conditions. Options (3) and (5) are incorrect because they use past-tense verbs (*had grown* and *grown*) to describe present conditions.

6. **(1) change got to gets** Option (1) correctly uses the present tense, which is consistent with the two previous sentences. Option (2) uses an incorrect form of the past perfect verb. Option (3) incorrectly uses the past perfect verb *had been* when the present tense is needed. Option (4) incorrectly uses the plural verb *are* with the singular subject *danger*. Option (5) uses the past-tense verb *got* when the present tense is needed.

7. **(5) bring** Option (5) correctly uses the present-tense verb *bring*. Options (1) and (2) incorrectly provide past-tense verbs when the present tense is needed. Option (3) uses an incorrect form of the word *bring*. Option (4) incorrectly uses the future tense (*will bring*).

8. **(4) occur** Option (4) correctly uses the present-tense verb *occur*, which is consistent with the present-tense verbs in the sentence. Option (1) incorrectly uses the past-tense verb, *occurred*. Option (2) incorrectly uses the past perfect verb *had occurred* for action in the present. Option (3) incorrectly changes the meaning of the sentence by adding the word *not*. Option (5) incorrectly uses a future perfect verb, *will have occurred,* for action in the present.

9. **(5) no correction is necessary** Option (5) is correct because the sentence is correct as written. Option (1) incorrectly uses the past-tense verb *were*, which is not consistent with the present-tense verbs in the sentence, *are* and *have*. Option (2) incorrectly uses a singular past-tense verb that is not consistent with the plural subject *Stings* or with the tense of the other verbs in the sentence. Option (3) incorrectly uses a past-tense verb, *had*, which is not consistent with the tense of the other verbs in the sentence. Option (4) incorrectly uses the singular verb *has* with the plural subject *people.*

KEY Skill 8 Subject-Verb Agreement
Pages 40–41

1. **(2) is** Option (2) is correct because the subject, *being sleepy*, is singular and requires the singular verb *is*, which retains the tense of the original sentence. Options (1) and (3) suggest the plural verbs *views* and *are*, which do not agree with the singular subject, *being sleepy*. Option (4) uses the past tense *was*, which changes the meaning of the original sentence. Option (5) is incorrect because it inserts *being* after the phrase *being sleepy behind the wheel* and would not make sense.

2. **(4) change increase to increases** Option (4) is correct because the compound subject has singular parts joined by *or* and requires a singular verb, *increases*. Option (1) incorrectly uses the verb *was*, a form that should not be used with the subject *you*. Option (2) is incorrect because it changes the present-tense verb form (*driving*) to a present-perfect form (*having driven*) that is not in agreement with the present-tense verb *increases*. Option (3) incorrectly uses the verb *is*, a form that should not be used with the subject *you*. Option (5) is not correct because the compound sentence has singular parts joined by *or* and requires a singular verb, not the plural verb *increase*.

3. **(2) are** Option (2) correctly pairs the plural verb *are* with the plural subject *danger signs*. Option (1) incorrectly uses the singular verb *is* with the plural subject. Option (3) incorrectly changes the verb to the past-tense form *were*, which does not agree with the present tense found elsewhere in the sentence (*are*). Option (4) is incorrect because the verb, *has been*, is a singular present-perfect form when a plural present form is needed. Option (5) unnecessarily uses the present perfect verb *have been* when the plural simple present form is needed.

4. **(3) change means to mean** Option (3) correctly uses the plural verb *mean* with a compound subject joined by *and*. Options (1) and (2) incorrectly use verb forms that should not be used with the subject *you*. Option (4) incorrectly substitutes the past-tense form of the verb (*meant*) and does not fix the

subject-verb agreement problem. Option (5) is not correct because the compound subject is joined by *and*, so it requires a plural verb, not the singular verb *means*.

5. **(5) change is to are** Option (5) is correct because the compound subject is joined by *and* and requires a plural verb, *are*. Option (1) incorrectly uses the past-tense verb *were*, which does not make sense with the rest of the paragraph. Option (2) incorrectly uses the singular past-tense verb *was*, which neither agrees with the subject nor makes sense with the rest of the paragraph. Option (3) incorrectly uses the present perfect verb *have been*, which does not make sense with the rest of the paragraph. Option (4) incorrectly uses a verb form, *am*, that should be used only when the subject is *I*.

6. **(4) serve** Option (4) is correct because the plural verb form *serve* agrees with the plural subject *They*. Option (1) incorrectly uses the singular verb *serves* with a plural subject. Option (2) uses an incorrectly formed future-tense verb, *will serves*. Options (3) and (5) are incorrect because they change the tense of the verb to tenses that are not consistent with the rest of the passage.

7. **(1) change are to is** Option (1) is correct because the compound subject has singular parts joined by *or* and requires a singular verb, *is*. Option (2) incorrectly uses the verb *am*, which should be used only when the subject is *I*. Option (3) incorrectly uses the plural past-tense verb *were*, which neither agrees with the singular subject nor is consistent with the rest of the paragraph. Option (4) incorrectly suggests the future-tense verb *shall be*, which does not make sense in the sentence. Option (5) is not correct because the compound sentence has singular parts joined by *or* and requires a singular verb, not the plural verb *are*.

8. **(1) are leavening agents, and they make** Option (1) correctly uses the plural verbs *are* and *make* with the plural subjects *substances* and *they*. Option (2) is incorrect because the singular verb *is* does not agree with the plural subject *substances*. Option (3) incorrectly uses the singular verbs *is* and *makes* with the plural subjects in the sentence. Option (4) is incorrect because the singular verb *makes* does not agree with the plural subject *they*. Option (5) incorrectly uses the past tense *made*, which is not consistent with the tense of the sentence or the rest of the paragraph.

9. **(2) change are to is** Option (2) is correct because the compound subject has singular parts joined by *nor*, and therefore it requires a singular verb. Option (1) incorrectly uses the present perfect *has been*, which unnecessarily changes the tense of the sentence. Option (3) incorrectly uses the plural present-perfect verb *have been*, which does not agree with the subject and also unnecessarily changes the meaning of the sentence. Option (4) incorrectly uses the verb *am*, which should be used only when the subject is *I*. Option (5) incorrectly uses the plural past-tense verb *were*, which does not agree with the subject.

Skill 9 Common Agreement Problems
Pages 44–45

1. **(3) change exists to exist** Option (3) is correct because the subject, *pitfalls*, is plural and requires a plural verb, *exist*. Option (1) incorrectly changes the plural *advantages* to its singular form, while the word *many* indicates that a plural noun is required. Option (2) incorrectly changes the plural *cards* to the singular *card*, which does not make sense in the sentence. Option (4) is incorrect because it changes the simple present-tense verb to a participial form (*existing*) that is not in agreement with the subject. Option (5) incorrectly uses the past-tense verb *existed*, which is not consistent with the present tense of the rest of the paragraph.

2. **(5) things we charge adds** Option (5) is correct because the subject, *cost*, is singular and requires a singular verb, *adds*. Option (1) is not correct because the singular subject is paired with the plural verb *add*. Option (2) creates an additional error in the sentence; the plural subject *we* requires a plural verb, not the singular *charges*. Option (3) incorrectly changes the plural *things* to *thing* while the word *many* indicates that a plural noun is needed. Option (4) incorrectly uses the past-tense verb *added*, which doesn't make sense in the sentence.

3. **(2) change There's to There are** Option (2) is correct because the subject, *many*, is plural and requires a plural subject, *are*. Option (1) incorrectly pairs the plural subject with the singular verb *is*. Option (3) incorrectly uses the past-tense verb *were*, which is not consistent with the rest of the paragraph. Option (4) is incorrect because changing *have* to *is* does not solve the agreement problem and does not make sense. Use of the past-tense verb *had* (option 5) likewise does not solve the agreement problem and changes the meaning of the sentence.

4. **(1) is** Option (1) is correct because the subject *Paying* requires a singular verb, *is*. Options (2) and (3) incorrectly use a past-tense verb, *was*, and future-tense verb, *will be*, both of which are inconsistent with the rest of the paragraph. Option (4) incorrectly pairs the singular subject with the plural verb, *are*. Option (5) incorrectly uses the present-perfect verb *has been*, which unnecessarily alters the meaning of the sentence.

5. **(2) do our financial situations suffer** Option (2) is correct because the subject, *situations*, is plural and requires a plural verb, *do*. Option (1) incorrectly pairs the plural subject with the singular verb *does*. Options (3) and (4) incorrectly use a past-tense verb, *did*, and future-tense verb, *will*, both of which are inconsistent with the rest of the paragraph. Option (5) is incorrect because *suffers* does not make sense in the sentence.

6. **(1) change are to is** Option (1) is correct because the singular subject *Korean War Veterans Memorial* requires the singular verb *is*. Option (2) is not correct because it uses a verb form, *be*, that does not make sense in the sentence. Option (3) incorrectly pairs the singular subject with the plural verb *were*. Options (4) and (5) are incorrect because they use past-tense verb forms that unnecessarily alter the meaning of the original sentence.

7. **(1) dedicated 42 years after the war's end, now reminds** Option (1) is correct because the subject, *Memorial*, is singular and requires a singular verb, *reminds*. Option (2) is incorrect because *dedicates* does not make sense in the sentence. Option (3) incorrectly pairs the singular subject with the plural verb *remind*. Options (4) and (5) are incorrect because neither *ends* nor *dedicating* make sense in the sentence.

8. (2) change <u>is</u> to <u>are</u> Option (2) correctly uses the plural verb *are*, which agrees with the plural subject *soldiers*. Option (1) incorrectly changes the singular *wall* to the plural *walls* while the article *a* indicates that a singular noun is required. Option (3) incorrectly uses the singular past-tense verb *was*, which neither agrees with the subject nor makes sense with the rest of the paragraph. Option (4) is incorrect because the past-tense verb *trudged* is not in agreement with the rest of the sentence. Option (5) incorrectly pairs the plural subject with the singular verb *is*.

9. (5) no correction is necessary Option (5) is correct because the sentence is correct as written. Option (1) incorrectly pairs the singular subject *inscription* with the plural verb *are*. Option (2) incorrectly uses the plural past-tense verb *were*, which neither agrees with the subject nor makes sense with the rest of the paragraph. Options (3) and (4) are incorrect because neither *engraves* nor *read* have a verb tense that agrees with the rest of the sentence.

KEY Skill 10 Pronouns
Pages 48–49

1. (4) our Option (4) is correct because the second-person pronoun *our* is consistent with the second-person pronoun *us* used previously in the sentence. Option (1) is incorrect because the third-person pronoun *their* is not consistent with the second-person pronoun *us*. Options (2) and (3) are incorrect because a possessive pronoun is required, not the object pronoun *them* or the subject pronoun *they*. Option (5) is incorrect because the singular pronoun *my* is not consistent with the plural pronoun *us*.

2. (3) replace <u>they</u> with <u>we</u> Option (3) is correct because *we* is consistent with the first-person pronouns in the sentence, *We* and *our*. Option (1) is incorrect because *You* is inconsistent with both the first-person pronoun *our* and the third-person pronoun *they*. Option (2) is incorrect because *your* is inconsistent with both the first-person pronoun *We* and the third-person pronoun *they*. Option (4) unnecessarily suggests replacing *a magazine* with *magazines,* which does nothing to make the pronouns consistent. Option (5) is incorrect because the third-person pronoun *they* is inconsistent with the first-person pronouns *We* and *our*.

3. (1) replace <u>Your</u> with <u>Our</u> Option (1) is correct because the first-person plural pronoun *Our* is consistent with the rest of the paragraph. Option (2) adds an unnecessary word to the sentence and does nothing to make the pronoun consistent. Options (3) and (4) incorrectly suggest the singular pronoun *My* and third-person pronoun *Their*, neither of which is consistent with the first-person plural pronouns used throughout the paragraph. Option (5) is incorrect because the second-person pronoun *Your* is not consistent with the rest of the paragraph.

4. (5) no correction is necessary Option (5) is correct because the sentence is correct as written. Options (1) and (2) incorrectly replace the second-person pronoun *you* with pronouns that are not consistent with the second pronoun in the sentence. Options (3) and (4) incorrectly replace the second-person pronoun *you* with pronouns that are not consistent with the first pronoun in the sentence.

5. (2) you and I Option (2) is correct because the first-person pronoun is part of the subject, so the subject pronoun *I* is

necessary. Option (1) is incorrect because a subject pronoun is needed, not the object pronoun *me*. Option (3) is incorrect because the third-person pronoun *they* is not consistent with the previous second-person pronoun *you*. Option (4) is incorrect because a subject pronoun is needed, not the possessive pronoun *yours*. Option (5) is incorrect because the first-person pronoun *I* is not consistent with the second-person pronoun already in the sentence, *you*.

6. (2) change <u>they</u> to <u>their</u> Option (2) correctly uses the possessive pronoun *their* to describe the children's parents. Option (1) is incorrect because a possessive pronoun is needed, not the object pronoun *them*. Option (3) is incorrect because a third-person pronoun is needed, not the second-person pronoun *our*. Option (4) is incorrect because a third-person possessive pronoun is needed, not the first-person object pronoun *us*. Option (5) is incorrect because a possessive pronoun is needed, not the subject pronoun *they*.

7. (2) change <u>him</u> to <u>he</u> Option (2) is correct because a subject pronoun is needed. *She and he* is the subject of the sentence. Option (1) is incorrect because a subject pronoun is needed, not the object pronoun *her*. Option (3) is incorrect because using the first-person pronoun *we* changes the meaning of the sentence. Option (4) only reverses the order of the pronouns without correcting the use of the object pronoun *him* as part of the subject of the sentence. Option (5) incorrectly uses the object pronoun *him* as part of the subject of the sentence.

8. (5) they do Option (5) correctly uses the plural subject pronoun *they* to refer to the antecedent *rules*. Option (1) incorrectly uses the singular pronoun *it* to refer to *rules*, which is plural. Options (2) and (3) are incorrect because neither *their* nor *there* make sense in the sentence as suggested. Option (4) incorrectly uses the possessive pronoun *its* where a subject pronoun is needed.

9. (3) we Option (3) is correct because the first-person plural pronoun *we* is consistent with the pronoun that begins the sentence. Options (1) and (2) incorrectly suggest pronouns that are not consistent with the first-person plural pronoun in the sentence.
Options (4) and (5) incorrectly suggest the possessive pronouns *your* and *their*, which do not make sense in the sentence with the first-person plural pronoun *we* that appears at the beginning of the sentence.

Skill 11 Pronouns and Antecedents
Pages 52–53

1. (5) you can Option (5) forms the clearest sentence by eliminating *they*, which has no clear antecedent. Option (1) is not the best because the pronoun *they* has no clear antecedent. Options (2), (3), and (4) are incorrect because the pronouns suggested are not consistent with the pronoun *you* used earlier in the sentence.

2. (3) remove <u>their</u> Option (3) creates the clearest sentence by eliminating *their*, which neither agrees with the antecedent *Anyone* nor is necessary. Option (1) is incorrect because *You* does not agree with *their* in person. Option (2) is incorrect because *they* is not a possessive pronoun. Option (4) is incorrect because *our* does not agree with *Anyone* in either person or number. Option (5) is incorrect because *their* does not agree in number with its antecedent, *Anyone*.

3. **(1) replace <u>they want</u> with <u>he or she wants</u>** Option (1) correctly uses singular pronouns *he* and *she*, which agree with the antecedent *writer*, the gender of whom is unspecified. Option (2) is incorrect because the second-person pronoun *you* does not work with the third-person antecedent, *a writer*. Options (3) and (4) do not address the error in agreement between the plural pronoun *they* and its singular antecedent, *a writer*. Option (5) is not correct because the plural *they* does not agree in number with the antecedent *writer*.

4. **(3) replace <u>it</u> with <u>the letter</u>** Option (3) forms the clearest sentence because it replaces the pronoun *it*, which has no antecedent, with a specific noun. Options (1) and (2) incorrectly replace one pronoun without an antecedent with another. Option (4) does not address the error, leaving *it* without an antecedent. Option (5) is incorrect because the pronoun *it* has no antecedent in the sentence.

5. **(5) no correction is necessary** Option (5) is correct because the sentence is correct as written. Option (1) unnecessarily changes the meaning of the sentence. Option (2) is not the best choice because the sentence begins by addressing the reader, so a shift to the first-person *we* is unnecessary and unclear. Option (3) unnecessarily changes the meaning of the sentence. Option (4) unnecessarily changes the meaning of the sentence by substituting the general *everyone* with the more specific *he and she*.

6. **(2) change <u>their</u> to <u>a</u>** Option (2) forms the clearest sentence by eliminating *their*, which neither agrees with the antecedent *Each* nor is necessary. Replacing the pronoun *their* with the pronoun *his* (option 1) is incorrect because the gender of the players is unspecified. Option (3) is incorrect because the plural subject *All* does not agree with the singular verb *is*. Option (4) is incorrect because the plural verb *are* does not agree with the singular subject *Each*. Option (5) is incorrect because the plural pronoun *their* does not agree with the singular antecedent *Each*.

7. **(4) each other, and when cards are dealt** Option (4) replaces the pronoun *it*, which has no antecedent, with a specific noun. Option (1) is incorrect because the pronoun *it* has no clear antecedent. Option (2) is incorrect because both *them* and *it* lack a clear antecedent. Option (3) replaces the singular pronoun *it* with the plural pronoun *they*, but the pronoun still lacks a clear antecedent. Option (5) is incorrect because the second-person pronoun *you* is not consistent with other nouns and pronouns in the paragraph.

8. **(1) change <u>They</u> to <u>The players</u>** Option (1) correctly replaces the pronoun *They*, which has no clear antecedent, with a specific noun. Options (2) and (3) each insert a pronoun without a clear antecedent into the sentence without clarifying the antecedent of *They*. Option (4) suggests the second-person pronoun *You*, which is not consistent with other nouns and pronouns used in the paragraph. Option (5) is incorrect because removing these words would make the sentence even more vague.

9. **(1) they said they would, or stop their opponents** Option (1) is correct because the plural pronouns *they* and *their* agree with the plural antecedent *partners*. Option (2) incorrectly uses singular pronouns to refer to the plural

partners. Option (3) includes a confusing shift from the third-person pronoun *they* to the first-person pronoun *our*. Option (4) incorrectly replaces the possessive pronoun *their* with the object pronoun *them*. Option (5) incorrectly uses the singular pronoun *he* to refer to the plural antecedent *partners*.

Skill 12 Apostrophes
Pages 56–57

1. **(4) change <u>agencys'</u> to <u>agency's</u>** Option (4) correctly forms the singular possessive noun by adding an apostrophe and *s* to the singular noun *agency*. Options (1) and (2) suggest incorrect changes to the placement of the apostrophe in *you've*, which is correct as is. Option (3) is incorrect because it does not make sense for *bills* to be made possessive in the context of the sentence. Option (5) is incorrect because the word *a* indicates that a singular noun is needed, not the plural possessive noun *agencies'*.

2. **(3) change <u>were'nt</u> to <u>weren't</u>** Option (3) corrects the contraction by placing the apostrophe where the *o* would be in *not*. Options (1) and (2) incorrectly replaces the subject of the sentence, *agencies*, with a possessive noun. Options (4) and (5) do not correctly place the apostrophe in the contraction *weren't*.

3. **(2) change <u>theyre</u> to <u>they're</u>** Option (2) corrects the contraction by placing the apostrophe where the *a* would be in *are*. Option (1) suggests an incorrect placement of the apostrophe in *they're*. Option (3) is incorrect because the possessive pronoun *their* does not make sense in the sentence. Option (4) is not correct because it omits the apostrophe from the contraction *they're* and adds another verb, which does not make sense as it would read *they are are*. Option (5) is incorrect because it omits the apostrophe from the contraction *they're*.

4. **(1) change <u>collector's</u> to <u>collectors'</u>** Option (1) is correct because the context of the sentence indicates that all collectors have restricted calling hours, and the correct form for a possessive plural noun is to add only an apostrophe: *collectors'*. Option (2) is incorrect because the plural noun *collectors* does not make sense in the sentence as a possessive plural noun is needed. Options (3) and (4) are not correct because it does not make sense for *hours* to be made possessive in this sentence. Option (5) is not correct because the context of the sentence indicates that more than one collector has restricted calling hours, so a plural possessive is needed, not the singular possessive *collector's*.

5. **(5) change <u>its</u> to <u>it's</u>** Option (5) provides the correct spelling of the contraction it is: *it's*. The apostrophe is placed where the *i* would be in *is*. Options (1) and (2) are incorrect because it does not make sense for *collectors* to be made possessive. Option (3) changes the meaning of the sentence by replacing the incorrectly spelled contraction for *it is* with the contraction for *is not*. Option (4) is incorrect because it shows an incorrect placement of the apostrophe in the contraction *it's*.

6. **(3) workers, a day's work won't** Option (3) correctly inserts the apostrophe in the contraction *won't*. Option (1) is not correct because it includes the contraction *won't* without an apostrophe. Option (2) is incorrect because it does not make sense for *workers* to be made possessive in the sentence. Option (4) is not correct because the contraction

won't has the apostrophe inserted in the wrong place. Option (5) is incorrect because it does not make sense for the possessive *day's* to be replaced with the plural *days*.

7. **(3) change <u>Our's</u> to <u>Ours</u>** Option (3) is correct because the possessive pronoun *Ours* does not need a apostrophe. Options (1) and (2) are incorrect because it does not make sense for *economics* to be made possessive. Option (4) incorrectly includes an apostrophe with the possessive pronoun *Ours*. Option (5) is incorrect because it does not make sense for the plural *days* to be replaced with the possessive *days'*.

8. **(2) change <u>job's</u> to <u>jobs'</u>** Option (2) is correct because the plural possessive form is needed, which is formed by adding an apostrophe to the end of the plural noun *jobs*. Option (1) is incorrect because it does not make sense for *sales* to be possessive. Options (3) and (4) are incorrect because in this sentence, it does not make sense for *hours* to be made possessive. Option (5) is incorrect because it does not make sense for *shifts* to be possessive.

9. **(2) change <u>womens'</u> to <u>women's</u>** Option (2) is correct because the plural possessive form is needed, which is formed by adding an apostrophe and *s* to the end of the irregular plural noun *women*. Option (1) is incorrect because it does not make sense for *positions* to be made possessive in this sentence. Option (3) incorrectly omits the apostrophe from *women's*. Options (4) and (5) are incorrect because *jobs* does not need to be made possessive in this sentence.

Skill 13   Commas in Sentences
Pages 60–61

1. **(3) insert a comma after <u>search</u>** Option (3) is correct because *search* is the last word of the first independent clause in this compound sentence. A comma must be inserted at the end of the first independent clause and before the connecting word *but*. Options (1) and (2) incorrectly suggest inserting a comma in the middle of the first independent clause. Option (4) incorrectly places the comma after *but* instead of before it. Option (5) is not correct because the suggested comma would interrupt the second independent clause.

2. **(2) resumé are your work history and your** Option (2) is correct because the connecting word *and* joins two nouns (*work history* and *education*), not two independent clauses, and therefore does not require a comma. Option (1) includes an unnecessary comma before a connecting word that joins two nouns. Options (3), (4), and (5) include commas in inappropriate places in a sentence that does not need any commas.

3. **(1) would personally fit in with the new company, and** Option (1), the original sentence, is correct because *company* is the last word of the first independent clause in this compound sentence, so a comma must be inserted before the connecting word *and*. Option (2) omits the necessary comma at the end of the first independent clause. Options (3) and (4) include commas that unnecessarily interrupt the first independent clause. Option (5) includes a comma after *and* instead of after the last word of the first independent clause.

4. **(1) insert a comma after <u>teamwork</u>** Option (1) is correct because *teamwork* is the last word of the first independent clause in this compound sentence, so a comma

must be inserted after *teamwork* and before the connecting word *so*. Option (2) incorrectly places the comma after the connecting word instead of before it. Options (3), (4), and (5) incorrectly suggest placing commas where they would interrupt the second independent clause.

5. **(4) remove the comma after <u>qualified</u>** Option (4) correctly removes the unnecessary comma from the independent clause in this complex sentence. Option (1) creates an error by inserting an unnecessary comma in a dependent clause. Option (2) removes a necessary comma at the end of the dependent clause that begins the sentence and leaves the unnecessary comma after *qualified* uncorrected. Option (3) correctly removes the unnecessary comma after *qualified*, but incorrectly inserts an unneeded comma after *address*. Option (5) correctly removes the unnecessary comma after *qualified*, but also incorrectly inserts an unnecessary comma after *meet*.

6. **(5) insert a comma after <u>store</u>** Option (5) is correct because *store* is the last word of the first independent clause in this compound sentence, so a comma must be inserted after *store* and before the connecting word *and*. Option (1) includes an unneeded comma in the first independent clause. Options (2) and (3) are not correct because the connecting word *or* joins two nouns and therefore does not need a comma either before or after it. Option (4) includes an unneeded comma in the first independent clause.

7. **(4) Because these people do not have checking accounts, they** Option (4) correctly places a comma at the end of the dependent clause (after *accounts*) to separate it from the independent clause. Options (1), (2), and (3) include unnecessary commas within the dependent clause in this complex sentence. Option (5) is incorrect because it does not include the comma needed at the end of the dependent clause that begins this complex sentence.

8. **(2) purchases and pays bills by writing checks instead of** Option (2) correctly removes the unnecessary comma. Because the dependent clause in this sentence comes at the end, it does not need to be separated from the independent clause by a comma. Option (1) is incorrect because the original sentence contains an unneeded comma before the dependent clause. Option (3) includes an unnecessary comma where the connecting word *and* joins two verbs. Option (4) includes an unnecessary comma in the independent clause, and option (5) includes an unnecessary comma in the dependent clause.

9. **(3) insert a comma after <u>use</u>** Option (3) correctly places a comma at the end of the dependent clause (after *use*) to separate it from the independent clause. The commas in options (1) and (2) both interrupt the dependent clause unnecessarily. Options (4) and (5) interrupt the independent clause with unnecessary commas.

Skill 14   Unnecessary Commas
Pages 64–65

1. **(3) remove the comma after <u>things</u>** Option (3) correctly removes the comma that separates the two verbs in the sentence, *accumulate* and *find*. Option (1) incorrectly inserts a comma between the subject, *Many*, and the verbs, *accumulate* and *find*. Option (2) correctly removes the

unneeded comma after *things* but also inserts an unnecessary comma between the two verbs in the sentence. Option (4) inserts an unnecessary comma between the two verbs in the sentence. Option (5) is not correct because the comma is not needed in the middle of the phrase *find it hard to throw anything away.*

2. **(4) remove the comma after <u>junk</u>** Option (4) correctly removes the comma after *junk,* which is the final item in a series and does not require a comma. Options (1), (2), and (3) incorrectly remove a comma that is needed to separate the items in the series (*old clothes, empty boxes, never-read magazines, and just plain junk*). Option (5) is not correct because the original sentence contains an unnecessary comma after the final item in a series.

3. **(1) through your home from top to bottom and to decide** Option (1), the original sentence, is correct; it requires no commas. Options (2), (3), and (4) incorrectly insert commas that unnecessarily separate the first verb *go* and the second verb *decide.* Option (5) is not correct because the comma is not needed in the verb phrase *decide what is really necessary.*

4. **(5) remove the comma after <u>twelve</u>** Option (5) correctly removes the comma that separates the subject of the clause, *ten or twelve,* and its verb, *are.* Option (1) incorrectly inserts a comma that separates the subject *boxes* from the verb *might be.* Option (2) incorrectly inserts a comma in the middle of the verb phrase *might be handy to keep.* Option (3) incorrectly removes the comma that separates the first independent clause from the second in this compound sentence. Option (4) incorrectly inserts a comma between the pair of nouns, *ten* and *twelve.*

5. **(5) no correction is necessary** The sentence is correct as written. Options (1) and (2) incorrectly remove the necessary commas after *recycle* and *away,* which separate the verbs in the series. Options (3) and (4) similarly remove the necessary commas, which separate the items in the series (*friends, family, or a charity*).

6. **(2) remove the comma after <u>apartment</u>** Option (2) correctly removes the unnecessary comma after *apartment,* which separates the subject, *Your house or apartment,* from the verb, *can be kept.* Option (1) incorrectly inserts a comma that would separate the nouns in the compound subject, *house or apartment.* Option (3) is incorrect because it includes the unnecessary comma after *apartment* and adds another unnecessary comma after *clutter.* Option (4) unnecessarily interrupts the verb phrase *acquire a few good habits* and retains the unnecessary comma after apartment. Option (5) is incorrect because it retains the unnecessary comma after *apartment* and adds another unnecessary comma after *few.*

7. **(4) closets and dressers once a year,** Option (4) correctly removes the unnecessary comma that separates the pair of nouns, *closets and dressers.* Option (1), the original sentence, is incorrect because it contains an unnecessary comma that separates the pair of nouns, *closets and dressers.* Option (2) retains the unnecessary comma after *closets* and adds another unnecessary comma after *dressers.* Option (3) removes the unnecessary comma after *closets* but inserts an unnecessary comma after *dressers.* Option (5) incorrectly removes the necessary comma after *year* but adds an

unnecessary comma that interrupts the phrase, *once a year.*

8. **(3) remove the comma after <u>calls</u>** Option (3) correctly removes the unnecessary comma that separates the pair of verbs, *calls and asks.* Option (1) inserts an unnecessary comma in the middle of the clause. Option (2) incorrectly inserts a comma that separates the subject *organization such as Goodwill* from the verb *calls.* Option (4) is not correct because it removes the comma that separates the dependent clause that begins the sentence from the independent clause. Option (5) is not correct because it inserts a comma in the middle of the verb *will have.* (*Will* is contracted with *you,* forming *you'll*).

9. **(2) Your home and your life** Option (2) correctly removes the comma that separates the nouns in the compound subject. Option (1) incorrectly uses a comma to separate the nouns in the compound subject. Option (3) also incorrectly includes a comma that separates the pair of nouns, *home* and *life,* and it also adds another unnecessary comma after *your.* Option (4) is not correct because the comma unnecessarily separates the possessive adjective *Your* from the noun it describes, *home.* Option (5) includes both an unnecessary comma after *Your* and a comma that unnecessarily separates the subject *Your home and your life* from the verb *will be.*

10. **(1) home will lead to a** The original was correct as written, so option (1) is the best choice. Option (2) is incorrect because it inserts a comma that breaks the verb phrase. Option (3) is incorrect because the comma unnecessarily separates the subject and the verb. Option (4) is incorrect because it separates the complete sentence into two incomplete sentences. Option (5) is incorrect because the comma is not needed after the verb phrase.

KEY Skill 15 Spelling Homonyms
Pages 68–69

1. **(3) replace <u>four</u> with <u>for</u>** Option (3) correctly replaces the number *four* with the preposition *for.* Option (1) incorrectly replaces the verb *lessen,* meaning "to make less," with the noun *lesson,* which does not make sense when used that way in the sentence. Option (2) incorrectly replaces the possessive pronoun *your* with the contraction *you're,* which does not make sense as it adds an unnecessary verb (*are*) to the sentence. Option (4) incorrectly replaces *heart* with *hart,* which is a kind of deer. Option (5), the original sentence, is not correct because it uses the number *four* where the preposition *for* is needed.

2. **(5) no correction is necessary** The original sentence is correct as written. Option (1) incorrectly replaces the verb *do* with the noun *due,* referring to something that is owed. Option (2) incorrectly replaces the verb *know* with the negative word *no,* which does not fit in this sentence. Option (3) incorrectly replaces the contraction *you're* with the possessive pronoun *your,* which implies an object of possession that is not provided in this sentence. Option (4) incorrectly replaces the negative word *not* with the noun *knot.*

3. **(2) replace <u>weigh</u> with <u>way</u>** Option (2) correctly replaces the verb *weigh* with the noun *way.* Option (1) uses the contraction *They're,* which would be equivalent to

beginning the sentence, "They are is a simple...," and it does not make sense to have the verbs *are* and *is* together in the same sentence. Option (3) incorrectly replaces *for*, which is a part of the phrase *for heart disease*, with the word *four*, which is a number and would not make sense in context. Option (4) changes the conditional word *whether* to the noun *weather*, which refers to outdoor conditions and therefore, does not make sense. Option (5) is not correct because it uses the contraction *you're*, and it does not make sense to have the verbs *are* and *have* together in the context of the sentence.

4. **(2) replace <u>whose</u> with <u>who's</u>** Option (2) correctly replaces the possessive pronoun *whose* with *who's*, the contraction for *who is*. Option (1) incorrectly replaces the preposition *For* with the number *Four*. Option (3) incorrectly replaces the noun *waist*, referring to part of the body between the ribs and the hips, with the noun *waste*, referring to something thrown away or not used. Option (4) incorrectly replaces the verb *be* with the noun *bee*, which does not make sense. Option (5) incorrectly replaces the adjective *greater* with the noun *grater*, which is a device for grating or cutting food into small pieces.

5. **(1) replace <u>due</u> with <u>do</u>** Option (1) correctly replaces the noun *due* with the verb *do*. Option (2) incorrectly changes the noun *role*, which refers to the function of something or the part played by an actor, to *roll*, which refers to a turn or bread, and does not make sense in the sentence. Option (3) is not correct because it uses the possessive pronoun *its* where the contraction *it's* is needed. Option (4) incorrectly replaces the adverb *too* with the number *two*. Option (5) incorrectly replaces the preposition *in* with the noun *inn*.

6. **(4) replace <u>there</u> with <u>their</u>** Option (4) is correct because the possessive pronoun *their* is needed. Option (1) incorrectly replaces the connecting word *or* with the noun *ore*, which refers to a mineral. Option (2) is not correct because it replaces the word *not* with the noun *knot*, which changes the meaning of the sentence. Option (3) incorrectly replaces the noun *weather*, referring to the topic of the paragraph, with the conditional word *whether*, which changes the meaning of the sentence. Option (5) is not correct because it replaces the noun *vanes* with the noun *veins*, referring to blood vessels, which changes the meaning of the sentence.

7. **(3) replace <u>sea</u> with <u>see</u>** Option (3) correctly replaces the noun *sea*, referring to a large body of water, with the verb *see*. Option (1) incorrectly replaces the preposition *in* with the noun *inn*, referring to a kind of hotel. Option (2) incorrectly suggests the adjective *wee*, meaning "very small," which changes the meaning of the sentence. Option (4) incorrectly replaces the noun *night* with the noun *knight*, referring to a medieval soldier. Option (5) incorrectly replaces *there* with the contraction *they're*, which changes the meaning of the sentence.

8. **(4) replace <u>peace</u> with <u>piece</u>** Option (4) correctly replaces the noun *peace*, referring to a state of calm, with the noun *piece*, meaning "a part or portion," which makes sense in the context of the sentence. Option (1) incorrectly replaces the adjective *stationary*, meaning "unmoving," with the noun *stationery*, which refers to writing paper. Option (2) incorrectly replaces the connecting word *or* with the noun *ore*. Option (3) incorrectly replaces the conditional word *whether* with the

noun *weather*. Option (5) does not make sense because it replaces the verb *break*, meaning "to tear off or come apart," with the verb *brake*, meaning "to stop."

9. **(3) replace <u>its</u> with <u>it's</u>** Option (3) correctly replaces the possessive pronoun *its* with *it's*, the contraction for *it is*. Option (1) does not make sense because it replaces the noun *counsel*, meaning "advice," with the noun *council*, which refers to a group of people gathered to make a decision or give advice. Option (2) is not correct because it replaces the conditional word *whether* with the noun *weather*, but the word *or* indicates a conditional is needed. Option (4) incorrectly replaces *to*, which is part of the verb *to rain*, with the adverb *too*, meaning "in addition." Option (5) incorrectly replaces *rain* with *reign*, which refers to the rule of a king or other ruler and has nothing to do with weather conditions.

KEY Skill 16 Topic Sentences
Pages 72–73

1. **(5) Identity thieves use stolen information in several ways.** Option (5) is the best choice because it provides a framework for understanding the rest of the paragraph, which tells several ways that identity thieves use stolen information. Options (1) and (2) repeat ideas from the first paragraph and do not directly relate to the ideas included in the second paragraph. Options (3) and (4) do not relate to the specific topic of the paragraph.

2. **(2) There are several things you can do to protect your identity.** Option (2) clearly states the topic of the paragraph, which includes examples of the things you can do to protect your identify. Option (1) tells about one detail from the paragraph instead of introducing its topic. Option (3) is not related to the topic of the paragraph. Option (4) provides another specific example of a way to protect oneself against identity theft, but it does not effectively introduce the overall topic of the paragraph. Option (5) is not correct because the paragraph needs a topic sentence that states its main point.

3. **(5) No correction is necessary.** Option (5) is correct because the first sentence of the paragraph already effectively introduces the paragraph. Option (1) would not effectively introduce the paragraph because the topic is not comparing previous and current ways of doing business. Option (2) repeats the topic of the previous paragraph, which does not directly relate to the topic of this one. Option (3) does not relate to the topic of the paragraph. Option (4) inaccurately restates a detail from the paragraph as an opinion that does not precisely match the fact in the paragraph.

4. **(1) The JetExpert printer is an inkjet printer intended for the home office.** Option (1) correctly identifies the topic of the paragraph so that readers understand what the subject is and can relate following information to it. Option (2) is not the best choice because the sentence is too narrow; there is more in the paragraph than just black-and-white or color printing capability. Options (3), (4), and (5) are also not the best choices, for they too contain specific details about the topic, rather than the topic itself.

5. **(4) The JetExpert's three printing modes make it one of the most versatile printers on the market.** Option (4) is correct because it summarizes the details of the three printing modes contained in the paragraph's other

sentences. This is an example of a topic sentence that does not lead the paragraph, but instead summarizes it. Options (1), (2), and (3) are incorrect because they are details of the three printing modes, but each sentence covers only one mode. Option (5) is incorrect because the paragraph does contain a topic sentence.

6. (3) The JetExpert printer has two paper trays. Option (3) correctly provides a simple but critical idea that the rest of the paragraph explains. There are two trays; the rest of the paragraph tells what they are, where they are, and what they do. Option (1) is incorrect because it discusses only one tray and would be confusing if placed at the beginning of the paragraph. Option (2) is incorrect because it also mentions only one of the two trays explained in the paragraph. Option (4) is not the best choice, because the paragraph is about paper trays, not printing capability. Option (5) is also incorrect because the remaining information in this paragraph is not about printer set-up.

Skill 17 Transition Words
Pages 76–77

1. (1) replace Similarly with Then Option (1) replaces *Similarly*, which incorrectly suggests a comparison between ideas in sentences 2 and 3, with *Then*, which correctly puts the ideas in sequence. Option (2) is not correct because *However* suggests a contrast between ideas in sentences 2 and 3, but there is no contrast. Option (3) is not correct because *For instance* suggests that sentence 3 presents an example of an idea presented in sentence 2, but it does not. Option (4) is not correct because *Meanwhile* inappropriately suggests that the actions described in sentences 2 and 3 happen at the same time, but they do not. Option (5) is not correct because *Similarly* suggests a comparison between ideas in sentences 2 and 3, but there is no comparison.

2. (4) Therefore, you should not share your ID or password with any other student. Option (4) correctly adds the transition *Therefore*, which indicates the cause-and-effect relationship between sentences 7 and 8. Option (1) is not correct because *However* suggests a contrast between ideas in sentences 7 and 8, but there is no contrast. Option (2) is not correct because *For example* suggests that sentence 8 presents an example of an idea presented in sentence 7, but it does not. Option (3) is not correct because *Second* suggests a sequence that does not exist between the ideas in sentences 7 and 8. Option (5) is not correct because sentence 8 lacks a transition to link the ideas in sentences 7 and 8.

3. (2) replace As a result with Next Option (2) replaces *As a result*, which incorrectly suggests a cause-and-effect relationship between ideas in sentences 12 and 13, with *Next*, which correctly puts the ideas in sequence. Option (1) is not correct because *Similarly* suggests a comparison between ideas in sentences 12 and 13, but there is no comparison. Option (3) is not correct because *For example* suggests that sentence 13 presents an example of an idea presented in sentence 12, but it does not. Option (4) is not correct because *Finally* suggests that sentence 13 presents the final action in a sequence, but it does not. Option (5) is not correct because *As a result* suggests a cause-and-effect relationship between ideas in sentences 12 and 13, but there

is no such relationship.

4. (4) Finally, click the OK button. Option (4) is correct because *Finally* indicates that clicking the OK button is the final action in a sequence. Options (1), (2), and (3) are incorrect because they suggest transitions that would not indicate the place of sentence 16 at the end of the sequence clearly established by the words *First* in sentence 12 and *Then* in sentence 14. Option (5) is not correct because sentence 16 needs a transition to link the action in that sentence to actions in previous sentences in the paragraph.

5. (3) replace The program with Otherwise, the program Option (3) is correct because *Otherwise* indicates that there is a contrast between the ideas in sentences 20 and 21. Option (1) is not correct because *First* suggests a sequence that does not exist between the ideas in sentences 20 and 21. Option (2) is not correct because *As a result* suggests a cause-and-effect relationship that does not actually exist between the ideas in sentences 20 and 21. Option (4) is not correct because *Now* inappropriately suggests a time relationship between the ideas in sentences 20 and 21. Option (5) is not correct because sentence 21 lacks a transition to show the contrast between the ideas in sentences 20 and 21.

6. (1) Also Option (1) correctly identifies the transition word *Also*. Options (2), (3), (4), and (5) are not correct because they do not name transition words.

7. (1) replace Don't with However, don't Option (1) is correct because *However* indicates that there is a contrast between the idea in sentence 28 and the idea in the previous sentence. Option (2) is incorrect because *For instance* suggests that sentence 28 presents an example of an idea presented in sentence 27, but it does not. Option (3) is incorrect because *Meanwhile* inappropriately suggests that the actions described in sentences 27 and 28 happen at the same time. Option (4) is incorrect because *First* suggests that the idea in sentence 28 is the first in a sequence of ideas, but it is not. Option (5) is incorrect because *Similarly* suggests a comparison between ideas in sentences 27 and 28, but there is no comparison.

KEY Skill 18 Irrelevant Sentences
Pages 80–81

1. (3) remove sentence 3 Option (3) is correct because the challenge of living on one's own is not directly relevant to the topic of the paragraph. Option (1) is incorrect because sentence 1 is the topic sentence and is therefore necessary. Options (2) and (4) are incorrect because sentences 2 and 4 provide relevant details about the value of a toolkit. Option (5) is incorrect because the paragraph is better without sentence 3.

2. (2) remove sentence 10 Option (2) is correct because a discussion of the many different kinds of hammers would take the paragraph away from its main topic, which is what to include in a toolkit. Option (1) is incorrect because sentence 8 suggests one item to include in a toolkit and is therefore relevant to the topic. Options (3) and (4) are incorrect because sentences 12 and 13 also suggest items to include in a toolkit and are therefore relevant to the topic. Option (5) is incorrect because the paragraph is better without sentence 10.

3. **(2) remove sentence 16** Option (2) correctly suggests removing sentence 16, which is both personal and off topic. Option (1) is incorrect because sentence 15 suggests an item to include in a toolkit and is therefore relevant to the topic. Option (3) is incorrect because defining what size wrench to get for the toolkit is relevant. Option (4) is incorrect because sentence 19 lists two other items to include in a toolkit and is therefore relevant to the topic. Option (5) is incorrect because the paragraph is better without sentence 16.

4. **(5) no revision is necessary** Option (5) is correct because all six sentences in the fifth paragraph give information about items to include in a toolkit and are therefore relevant to the topic. Options (1), (2), (3), and (4) are incorrect because they each suggest removing sentences that give relevant information about items to include in a toolkit.

5. **(2) remove sentence 3** Option (2) is correct because although imagination is indeed important in a child, this comment is not directly relevant to the topic, which is reading to your child. Option (1) is incorrect because sentence 2 answers the question posed by the first sentence and is therefore relevant. Options (3) and (4) are incorrect because sentences 4 and 6 elaborate in a relevant way on the topic of doing something valuable for your child. Option (5) is incorrect because the paragraph is better without sentence 3.

6. **(5) no revision is necessary** Option (5) is correct because all four sentences in the second paragraph give relevant reasons why reading aloud to your child is valuable. Options (1), (2), (3), and (4) are incorrect because they each suggest removing sentences that give relevant information supporting the main idea, *why reading aloud to your child is valuable*.

7. **(3) remove sentence 22** Option (3) is correct because the quality of the artwork in children's books is not directly relevant to the topic of the paragraph, which tells how to read to your child. Option (1) is incorrect because sentence 18 gives an example relevant to sentence 17. Option (2) is incorrect because sentence 19 gives information relevant to the topic of how to read to your child. Option (4) is incorrect because sentence 24 elaborates in a relevant way on the idea in sentence 23. Option (5) is incorrect because the paragraph is better without sentence 22.

8. **(2) remove sentence 26** Option (2) is correct because it suggests removing an irrelevant personal remark. Option (1) is incorrect because it suggests removing the topic sentence of the paragraph. Options (3) and (4) are incorrect because they suggest removing sentences that relate directly to the topic of rewards of reading to children. Option (5) is incorrect because the paragraph is better without sentence 26.

KEY Skill 19 **Text Divisions Within Paragraphs**
Pages 84–85

1. **(2) sentence 5.** Option (2) is correct because sentence 5 introduces a new topic, the current status of the company, and should begin a new paragraph. Option (1) is incorrect because sentence 4 provides a conclusion to the ideas in the previous sentences and should not be separated from them. Options (3) and (4) are incorrect because sentences 7 and 8 are related to the previous sentences and therefore, do not

begin a new topic. Option (5) is not the best choice because the paragraph would be improved if divided in two.

2. **(3) move the sentence to the beginning of paragraph B** Option (3) is correct because sentence 9 introduces the information discussed in paragraph B. Option (1) is not the best choice because it is better to keep sentence 9 as the introduction to paragraph B than to delete it. Option (2) is incorrect because the sentence would make no sense if moved to the beginning of the memorandum, before the situation is explained. Option (4) is incorrect because sentence 9 functions better as an introduction than a conclusion to paragraph B. Option (5) is not correct because the sentence sounds like an introduction and would serve better at the beginning of paragraph B.

3. **(1) move the sentence to follow sentence 10** Option (1) is correct because sentence 15 provides more details about the technical specialists discussed in sentence 10. Options (2) and (3) are not good choices because sentences 11 and 12 discuss the spouses of the technical specialists, so following either sentence with details about the specialists would be confusing. Option (4) is incorrect because sentence 19 discusses the needs of support staff, so following with details about technical specialists would not make sense. Option (5) is incorrect because sentence 15 makes more sense after sentence 10 than it does in its current placement.

4. **(4) sentence 16.** Option (4) is correct because sentence 16 introduces a new topic: the problems of new support staff. Options (1), (2), and (3) are not good choices because each suggests beginning a new paragraph with a detail sentence that should not be separated from the others. Option (5) is incorrect because the paragraph would be improved if divided in two.

5. **(2) move the sentence to follow sentence 24** Option (2) is correct because the information about who will coordinate the program flows best after the description of the program. Option (1) is not the best choice because sentence 22 would not be a suitable introduction to the paragraph. Option (3) is not the best choice because sentence 25 refers to the costs of the program rather than to how the program will be run. Option (4) is not the best choice because sentence 26 refers to the proposal attached to the memorandum, so following with a detail about the proposal would be confusing. Option (5) is incorrect because sentence 22 makes more sense after sentence 24 than it does in its current placement.

6. **(4) sentence 27.** Option (4) is correct because sentence 27 introduces a new topic, requesting follow-up communication. Options (1), (2), and (3) are not good choices because each suggests beginning a new paragraph with a detail sentence that should not be separated from the others. Option (5) is not the best choice because the paragraph would be improved if divided in two.

7. **(1) delete the sentence** Option (1) is correct because sentence 29 adds nothing new to the memo and is best deleted. Options (2), (3), and (4) are incorrect because they suggest placing the sentence in paragraphs where it is unnecessary and not connected to the topics of those paragraphs. Option (5) is not the best choice because sentence 29 is unnecessary and best deleted.

1. **(4) move sentence 4 to the beginning of the paragraph** Option (4) is correct because sentence 4 is the topic sentence and is best placed at the beginning of the paragraph. Options (1) and (2) are not correct because sentence 1 introduces the ideas that follow in sentences 2 and 3 and should not be removed or moved. Option (3) is not correct because sentence 3 gives an example that adds to the meaning of the paragraph and should not be removed. Option (5) is not correct because the position of the topic sentence at the end of the paragraph does not make sense.

2. **(2) Insurance companies use two indicators to identify and rate treacherous intersections.** Option (2) most specifically tells the reader what information to expect in the paragraph. Option (1) relates to the paragraph but does not direct readers to what is coming in the paragraph as specifically as option (2). Options (3) and (4) are not correct because they do not adequately tell readers what to expect in the paragraph. Option (5) is not correct because the paragraph needs a topic sentence that states its main point.

3. **(4) combine paragraphs C and D** Option (4) is correct because the ideas in the two paragraphs are related and flow together smoothly; sentences 9 through 13 all support the topic sentence, sentence 8. Options (1) and (2) are not correct because they both suggest moving the topic sentence, sentence 8, to inappropriate places. Option (3) is not correct because sentence 13 gives an example that adds to the meaning of the paragraph and should not be removed. Option (5) is not the best answer because the content of the paragraphs is related and the paragraphs are better combined.

4. **(2) move the sentence to follow sentence 14** Option (2) is correct because sentence 17 supports and directly relates to the topic sentence, sentence 14. Option (1) is incorrect because sentence 14 is the topic sentence, and placing sentence 17 before it does not make sense. Option (3) is not correct because placing sentence 17 after sentence 15 would not make the best sense; the idea in sentence 17 most directly follows sentence 14. Option (4) is not correct because sentence 17 does not belong in paragraph F as well as it does in paragraph E. Option (5) is not correct because the placement of sentence 17 at the end of paragraph E does not make the best sense; the idea in sentence 17 most directly follows sentence 14.

5. **(1) combine paragraphs F and G** Option (1) is correct because the ideas in the two paragraphs are related and flow together smoothly; sentences 19 through 26 all support the topic sentence, sentence 18. Option (2) is not correct because sentence 18 is the topic sentence and makes the most sense at the beginning of paragraph F. Option (3) is incorrect because sentence 20 provides an important example and should not be removed. Option (4) is not correct because sentence 24 supports sentence 23, and together the two sentences provide an important example. Option (5) is not correct because the content of the paragraphs is related, so the paragraphs are better combined.

6. **(5) no revision is necessary** Option (5) is correct because the paragraph has a topic sentence and enough supporting sentences and does not need revision. Option (1) is not correct because sentence 27 is the topic sentence and makes the most sense at the beginning of the paragraph. Options (2), (3), and (4) are not correct because the sequence of ideas from sentence to sentence in the original paragraph H already makes sense, and removing sentences or moving them would disrupt this flow of ideas.

Pretest Answer Sheet: Language Arts, Writing

Name: _____ Class: _____ Date: _____

1 ①②③④⑤	5 ①②③④⑤	9 ①②③④⑤	13 ①②③④⑤	17 ①②③④⑤
2 ①②③④⑤	6 ①②③④⑤	10 ①②③④⑤	14 ①②③④⑤	18 ①②③④⑤
3 ①②③④⑤	7 ①②③④⑤	11 ①②③④⑤	15 ①②③④⑤	19 ①②③④⑤
4 ①②③④⑤	8 ①②③④⑤	12 ①②③④⑤	16 ①②③④⑤	20 ①②③④⑤

© 2009 Steck-Vaughn, an imprint of HMH Supplemental Publishers Inc. Permission granted to reproduce for classroom use.

Pretest Answer Sheet   123

Name: _____ Class: _____ Date: _____

Time Started: _____

Time Finished: _____

1 ①②③④⑤	6 ①②③④⑤	11 ①②③④⑤	16 ①②③④⑤	21 ①②③④⑤
2 ①②③④⑤	7 ①②③④⑤	12 ①②③④⑤	17 ①②③④⑤	22 ①②③④⑤
3 ①②③④⑤	8 ①②③④⑤	13 ①②③④⑤	18 ①②③④⑤	23 ①②③④⑤
4 ①②③④⑤	9 ①②③④⑤	14 ①②③④⑤	19 ①②③④⑤	24 ①②③④⑤
5 ①②③④⑤	10 ①②③④⑤	15 ①②③④⑤	20 ①②③④⑤	25 ①②③④⑤

USE A BALLPOINT PEN TO WRITE YOUR ESSAY

Name: _____

_____

_____

_____

_____

_____

_____

_____

_____

_____

_____

_____

_____

_____

_____

_____